Nikita Mikhalkov:
Between Nostalgia and Nationalism

KINOfiles Filmmakers' Companions
General Editor: Richard Taylor

Written for cineastes and students alike, and building on the achievements of the KINOfiles Film Companions, the KINOfiles Filmmakers' Companions are readable, authoritative, illustrated companion handbooks to the most important and interesting people who have participated in Russian cinema from its beginnings to the present. Each KINOfile examines the career of one filmmaker, or group of filmmakers, in the context of both Russian and world cinema. KINOfiles also include studies of people who have been active in the cinemas of the other countries that once formed part of the Soviet Union, as well as of émigré filmmakers working in the Russian tradition.

KINOfiles form a part of KINO: The Russian Cinema Series.

Filmmakers' Companions:

1	*Nikita Mikhalkov*	Birgit Beumers
2	*Alexander Medvedkin*	Emma Widdis
3	*Dmitri Shostakovich*	John Riley
4	*Kira Muratova*	Jane A. Taubman

Film Companions:

1	*The Battleship Potemkin*	Richard Taylor
2	*The Man with the Movie Camera*	Graham Roberts
3	*Burnt by the Sun*	Birgit Beumers
4	*Repentance*	Denise Youngblood and Josephine Woll
5	*Bed and Sofa*	Julian Graffy
6	*Mirror*	Natasha Synessios
7	*The Cranes Are Flying*	Josephine Woll
8	*Little Vera*	Frank Beardow
9	*Ivan the Terrible*	Joan Neuberger
10	*The End of St. Petersburg*	Vance Kepley, Jr.
11	*Chapaev*	Julian Graffy
12	*Storm over Asia*	Amy Sargeant

NIKITA MIKHALKOV: BETWEEN NOSTALGIA AND NATIONALISM

BIRGIT BEUMERS

KINOfiles Filmmakers' Companion 1

Published in 2005 by I.B.Tauris & Co. Ltd
6 Salem Road, London W2 4BU
175 Fifth Avenue, New York NY 10010
ibtauris.com

Copyright © Birgit Beumers, 2005

The right of the author of this work to be identified has been asserted by her in accordance with the Copyright, Designs and Patents Act 1988.

All rights reserved. Except for brief quotations in a review, this book, or any part thereof, may not be reproduced, stored in or introduced into a retrieval system, or transmitted, in any form or by any means, electronic, mechanical, photocopying, recording or otherwise, without the prior written permission of the publisher.

ISBN 1 86064 785 5
EAN 978 1 86064 785 7

A full CIP record for this book is available from the British Library

Typeset in Calisto by Dexter Haven Associates Ltd, London

Contents

Illustrations	vii
Acknowledgements and Transliteration	ix
Introduction	1
1 Nikita Mikhalkov: The 'Father' of the Nation?	3
2 Dreams of a Better Life: 1963–1975	13
3 'Retro' as Style: 1975–1980	40
4 Modern Times: 1980–1985	67
5 Between East and West: 1985–1991	81
6 Russia's Past in the Present: 1991–1999	99
Concluding Remarks	122
Notes	129
Filmography	137
Bibliography	145

Illustrations

1. *I Walk Around Moscow*, Kolka (Nikita Mikhalkov) and Alena (Galina Polskikh).   15
2. *At Home Among Strangers*, Brylov (Nikita Mikhalkov).   24
3. *Slave of Love*, Voznesenskaya (Elena Solovei).   31
4. *An Unfinished Piece for a Mechanical Piano*, Sergei (Yuri Bogatyrev) and Glagoliev (Nikolai Pastukhov).   44
5. *An Unfinished Piece for a Mechanical Piano*, Sashenka (Evgeniya Glushenko) and Platonov (Alexander Kaliagin).   48
6. *Five Evenings*, Tamara (Liudmila Gurchenko).   55
7. *A Few Days from the Life of I.I. Oblomov*, Zakhar (Andrei Popov), Oblomov (Oleg Tabakov) and Alexeyev (Avangard Leontiev).   59
8. *A Few Days from the Life of I.I. Oblomov*, Oblomov (Oleg Tabakov) and Stolz (Yuri Bogatyrev).   61
9. *Kinfolk*, Yuri Nikolayevich (Andrei Petrov) and Maria (Nonna Mordiukova).   72
10. *Private Conversation*, Ulianov and Kupchenko.   79
11. *Dark Eyes*, Romano (Marcello Mastroianni) and the vet Kostia (Dmitri Zolotukhin) on the cart.   87
12. *Urga*, Gombo and Pagma playing with the 'urga'.   94
13. *Burnt by the Sun*, lunch at the dacha: Vsevolod Konstantinovich (Viacheslav Tikhonov), Mitia (Oleg Menshikov), the aunts and Marusia (Ingeborga Dapkunaite); Nadia and Kotov with their backs to the camera.   106

14 *Burnt by the Sun*, Kotov (Nikita Mikhalkov) and Nadia (Nadia Mikhalkova) in the boat.   111

15 *The Barber of Siberia*, Tolstoy (Oleg Menshikov) and Jane (Julia Ormond) in the train.   116

16 *The Barber of Siberia*, McCracken (Richard Harris) and his invention.   119

Credits

Photos 1 and 3–11 by Anatoli Pashvykin; numbers 13 and 14 by Nikolai Gnesiuk; numbers 15 and 16 by Igor Gnevashev. Photos 2 and 12 are from the album *Nikita* and are reproduced here with the kind permission of TriTe.

Cover illustration courtesy of the Museum of Cinema, Moscow.

Acknowledgements and Transliteration

I would like to thank Anatoli Ermilov, Leonid Vereshchagin and Nikita Mikhalkov at TriTe, Natalia Chernova at the Library of the Film Institute, Moscow, and Philippa Brewster at I.B. Tauris, London. I am grateful to Julian Graffy and Richard Taylor for their comments on the draft of this book; to Nancy Condee for sharing her ideas on Mikhalkov's nationalism with me; and to Stephen Hutchings at the University of Surrey for organising a wonderful conference on screen adaptations. The Arts Faculty Research Fund at Bristol University and the Arts and Humanities Research Board have supported my work by funding research in Moscow and freeing up some of my time. For the illustrations I am deeply indebted to Igor Gnevashev, Nikolai Gnesiuk and Anatoli Pashvykin.

Transliteration from the Cyrillic to the Latin alphabet is a perennial problem for writers on Russian subjects. I have opted for a dual system. In the text I have used the Library of Congress system (without diacritics), but I have broken from this system (a) when a Russian name has a clear English version (e.g. Maria instead of Mariia, Alexander instead of Aleksandr); (b) when a Russian name has an accepted English spelling, or when Russian names are of Germanic origin (e.g. Yeltsin instead of Eltsin; Eisenstein instead of Eizenshtein); (c) when a Russian surname ends in -ii or -yi this is replaced by a single -y (e.g. Dostoevsky instead of Dostoevskii), and all Christian names end in a single -i; (d) when 'ia' or 'iu' are voiced (at the beginning of a word and when preceded by a vowel) they are rendered as 'ya' or 'yu' (e.g. Daneliya, Yuri) – with the sole addition of the name Asya, to avoid confusion with the continent, Asia. In the scholarly apparatus I have adhered to the Library of Congress system (with diacritics) for the specialist.

Introduction

Nikita Mikhalkov is without doubt one of the best known Russian film-makers. His name is familiar to most people interested in the cinema, not only Soviet and Russian cinema, last but not least thanks to his Oscar award for *Burnt by the Sun*, which has a volume in the KINOfile series devoted to it. Mikhalkov comes from a prestigious Soviet-Russian family and has played an important role in public life in the post-Soviet period. His films cover a range of historical periods and film genres. His career stretches from Khrushchev's Thaw, through the Brezhnev years of stagnation, to Gorbachev's perestroika and the post-Soviet period, thus offering scope for an exploration of Russia's cultural and cinematic life of the second half of the twentieth century.

Mikhalkov belongs to the mainstream of Soviet and Russian cinema rather than auteur cinema; this partly explains the relative lack of critical attention to the body of his work when compared with the auteur film-maker Andrei Tarkovsky. Furthermore, Mikhalkov never experienced serious difficulties with the Soviet authorities, and was therefore often perceived as an 'official' artist at times when dissident artists aroused greater interest from Western critics. The fact that Mikhalkov never had problems with the censorship – at least, none of his films was banned – was often attributed to his highly privileged Soviet family background. Yet his elder brother, Andrei Konchalovsky, who emigrated to the United States in the 1980s, did not benefit from such alleged protection; Konchalovsky's film *Asya's Happiness* [1967, released 1988] was shelved shortly after its completion in 1967. Mikhalkov has always been a controversial figure, swivelling between officialdom and the intelligentsia's dissidence, between popular and auteur cinema, between patriotism and nationalism, artist and prophet, storyteller and moralist, director and public figure, aesthete and politician. It is this ambiguity that makes Mikhalkov a figure who is admired and shunned at once, savaged by the critics and loved by audiences, despised by some colleagues and revered by others. Finally, he is one of the three Soviet/Russian directors – alongside Sergei Bondarchuk (*War and Peace*, 1968) and Vladimir Menshov (*Moscow Does Not Believe in Tears*, 1980) – to have won an Academy Award (Oscar) for *Burnt by the Sun* [1994] since the category of Foreign Language Film was established in 1956.

This book covers Mikhalkov's work as actor, scriptwriter and film-maker in chronological order. The discussion of the films offers a detailed account of the narratives while dwelling on important themes and cinematic devices, before proceeding to the overall significance of a given film in the corpus of Mikhalkov's work and in the cultural context. Particular emphasis is placed on the creation of a national space and the nostalgia related to Russia's or the Soviet Union's past.

The overall argument of this volume is that Mikhalkov performs a shift from a nostalgia for a past that is openly constructed as a myth to a nostalgia for a past that pretends to be authentic. I contend that this move is a result of the collapse of the Soviet value system – a system that encouraged myth making – and the director's inability to face up to the reality of the 1990s, when he turned both past and present into a myth that he himself mistook for real and authentic. Thus Mikhalkov's films of the 1990s feed into the longing for the myth making of the past that was a major driving force in popular taste in the post-Soviet period, placing Mikhalkov firmly within the popular mainstream but outside the field of innovative film-making – a move clearly acknowledged by the director himself with his attempt to make a blockbuster with *The Barber of Siberia*.

1. Nikita Mikhalkov: The 'Father' of the Nation?

Bio-Filmographical

Nikita Sergeyevich Mikhalkov was born on 21 October 1945 in Moscow into a family belonging to the Soviet intelligentsia. His father Sergei Vladimirovich (b. 1913) is a poet and playwright; he wrote (with Garold El-Registan) the text of the Soviet national anthem (1943, second version 1977), which he revised when the tune was brought back as the national anthem of the Russian Federation in 2000. Sergei Mikhalkov is one of the most popular authors of children's literature. Nikita Mikhalkov's mother, the writer and poet Natalia Petrovna Konchalovskaya (1903–1988), was the daughter of the painter Petr P. Konchalovsky (1876–1956). Konchalovskaya had a solid artistic background, going back into the nineteenth century: her mother, Olga V. Surikova, was the daughter of the famous painter Vasili I. Surikov (1848–1916). An earlier marriage of the film-maker's mother, Natalia, had produced a daughter, Ekaterina A. Bogdanova (b. 1931), who married Yulian S. Semenov, the novelist and author of the spy thriller *Seventeen Moments of Spring*. Under the Soviet system, the family changed the stress on the name from Mikhálkov to Mikhalkóv to hide their aristocratic background. Since the collapse of the Soviet Union Mikhalkov has shown excessive pride in the genealogy of his family, altering the stress back to Mikhálkov and producing a family tree that goes back over 200 years and connects the family to the painter Surikov, to the writers Pushkin, Tolstoy, Odoevsky and Gogol, and to Catherine the Great.

Mikhalkov's elder brother, Andrei (family pet-name Andron) (Mikhalkov-) Konchalovsky (b. 1937), is also a film-maker. His films *The First Teacher* [Pervyi uchitel', 1965], *Asya's Happiness* [Asino schast'e], originally called *The Story of*

Asya Kliachina, Who Loved but Did Not Marry [Istoriia Asi Kliachinoi, kotoraia liubila da ne vyshla zamuzh, 1967, released 1988], *A Nest of Gentlefolk* [Dvorianskoe gnezdo, 1969], based on Ivan Turgenev's novel, *Uncle Vania* [Diadia Vania, 1971], based on Anton Chekhov's play, *A Romance about Lovers* [Romans o vliublennykh, 1974] and the epic *Siberiade* [1979] constitute his filmography before his emigration in 1980. In some of these early films the younger brother Nikita appears as an actor (*Siberiade* and *A Nest of Gentlefolk*). Konchalovsky left the Soviet Union to work in Hollywood, where he successfully continued film-making.[1] Since the early 1990s he has again been working in Russia, making his sequel to *Asya's Happiness*, entitled *The Little Speckled Hen* [Kurochka Riaba, 1994]. In 1997 he took on the artistic direction of the celebrations for the 850th anniversary of Moscow. His film *House for Fools* [Dom durakov, 2002] was premiered at the Venice Film Festival 2002.

Mikhalkov is a child of the victory year 1945: born in the immediate aftermath of the war, he grew up during the last decade of Stalin's rule and spent his adolescence in a cultural climate that reflected relaxation after Stalin's purges and the hardship of the war. Mikhalkov went to the school of the Moscow Conservatory, specialising in the piano, until he transferred to an ordinary school for the last three years, during which time he took part in an acting group in the studio of the Stanislavsky Theatre. By this time the Khrushchev Thaw (1956–1964) was well under way: Khrushchev had delivered his 'secret speech', denouncing Stalin's crimes, and a period of liberalisation had begun in the arts, and in the theatre in particular. From 1963 onwards Nikita Mikhalkov trained as an actor at the Shchukin School, a theatre school attached to the Vakhtangov Theatre in Moscow. It was from this school that a group of graduates, together with their teacher Yuri Liubimov, had started off the Taganka Theatre, which pushed the limits of permissible theatrical production in the late 1960s and 1970s. Having been expelled in 1967 from the Shchukin School for absenting himself from classes in order to film, and, armed with a recommendation from the film-maker Georgi Daneliya, who had directed young Nikita in *I Walk Around Moscow* [Ia shagaiu po Moskve, 1963], Mikhalkov transferred to the All-Union State Institute for Cinematography (VGIK) to study directing under Mikhail Romm.[2] He graduated from the All-Union State Film Institute (hereafter Film Institute) in 1971 with his diploma film *A Quiet Day at the End of the War* [1970]. Mikhalkov had begun his career as an actor in the 1960s, and continued to appear in films after graduating as a film director. During the late 1960s and early 1970s he made a number of short films for the *Fitil'* ('Fuse') series,[3] short satirical clips used as trailers in cinemas. He also began scriptwriting, and after completing the script for *At Home Among Strangers* he was drafted into the army and served in the Pacific fleet and on the Kamchatka peninsula.

Nikita Mikhalkov: The 'Father' of the Nation?

After his army service he made his first feature, *At Home Among Strangers, a Stranger at Home* [1974], followed by *Slave of Love* [1975], both set in the years immediately following the Revolution. *An Unfinished Piece for a Mechanical Piano* [1977] bore testimony to Mikhalkov's talent for literary adaptation by presenting a version of an early Anton Chekhov play, frequently referred to under the title *Fatherlessness* [Bezottsovshchina, ca. 1878]. Adaptations of Alexander Volodin's *Five Evenings* [1978] and Ivan Goncharov's *Oblomov* [1979] followed. *Kinfolk* [1981] and *A Private Conversation* [1983] dealt with life in contemporary Russia. Mikhalkov thus moved in his films from the Revolution through the classical heritage and the post-war period towards the portrayal of the present. His growing reputation, nationally and internationally, led to the Italian production of *Dark Eyes* [1987], another adaptation of Chekhov, followed by *Hitchhike* [1990]. At a time when Tarkovsky chose to remain in Italy, Mikhalkov was representing Soviet cinema in an international project.

In 1991 he directed the French–Soviet co-production *Urga*, which won the Golden Lion at the Venice Film Festival in the same year, and was nominated for the Academy Award in 1993. *Burnt by the Sun* [1994] won the Grand Prix at the Cannes Film Festival in 1994 and the Oscar for Best Foreign Language Film in 1995.[4] Finally, *The Barber of Siberia* [1998], the most expensive Russian film with a $45 million budget, opened the Cannes Film Festival in 1999, an honour rarely accorded to a Russian director. Although the film was not entered in competition in any major festival, it was extremely popular with Russian audiences, but it did not fare well commercially in international distribution. In post-Soviet Russia Mikhalkov has climbed the ladder into the international market.

Public Life

Apart from being a very talented actor and a film-maker of international standing, Mikhalkov has also occupied, and continues to occupy, several influential positions in Russian cultural politics: in the early 1990s he acted as government adviser on cultural issues; in 1991 he joined the UNESCO Commission for Culture; and in 1993 he was elected president of the Russian Culture Foundation. He stood for election to parliament in the government party 'Russia, Our Home' in 1995, winning a seat that he later declined. He runs his own production company, TriTe, with its publishing arm 'Russian Archive'. In 1997 Mikhalkov was elected chairman of the Film-makers' Union (FU), a post in which he attempted to provide guidance and authority to a union that was crumbling, concerned only with its properties, social and medical services for its members, and care for the old, while urgent issues of authors' rights, distribution and copyright, as well as artistic concerns remained beyond the union's horizon.

Mikhalkov thus seeks the public arena and likes to cast himself in roles of power, although the positions he achieves do not always hold the power they seem to promise: the chairmanship of the Russian Culture Foundation is certainly prestigious, but time-consuming; a seat in parliament was declined because of a lack of time; the chairmanship of the Union has raised problems more than it endows power; and the presidency of the Moscow Film Festival is, above all, a representative function. Whenever Mikhalkov has sought positions of real power, he has failed: he was unable to place the man of his choice at the head of Goskino (the Russian State Committee of Cinematography); he could not stop the merger of Goskino with the Ministry of Culture; and he has never stood for presidential elections, although he genuinely seemed to believe in a possible nomination. As a public figure Mikhalkov is popular, yet surrounded by controversy. Mikhalkov's films and public statements testify to his views on national identity, on society and the individual, and on East and West. Cinematically, he has used a number of innovative devices, without ever revolutionising cinema on a grand scale. His films are well made, professionally impeccable, and always interesting to both audiences of auteur cinema and popular cinema; they are mainstream, tending towards blockbuster status in the 1990s. By attempting to strike the balance between commercial and art-house cinema Mikhalkov has found little support from Russian critics at a time when they clearly favoured pure auteurism instead of mass appeal; the intelligentsia-run film journals in particular dislike him both as a public figure and as a film-maker.

In the mid-1980s Mikhalkov had been – apart from Andrei Tarkovsky and Andrei Konchalovsky, both of whom had already emigrated – the only Soviet director with international connections. In 1986 he began filming *Dark Eyes* with Marcello Mastroianni in Italy, and he went on to make the Fiat-sponsored *Hitchhike* in 1990. After these international co-productions Mikhalkov had gathered enough experience, renown and contacts in Europe to set up his own film studio, TriTe. TriTe (Three Ts) stand for 'trud, tovarishchestvo, tvorchestvo' ('work, comradeship, creativity'). The company has a publishing arm called 'Russian Archive', which has published archival documents relating to Russian history.[5] In the establishment of this publishing arm Mikhalkov manifested his concern for Russian heritage, which is also reflected in the choice of the slogan for his studio, drawing on the concept of 'tovarishchestvo'. This term applies to both nineteenth-century management structures[6] and the Soviet-style comradeship that the Bolsheviks introduced with the address 'tovarishch'. TriTe produces Mikhalkov's films, assists foreign film production (in facilitating the hire of studios and organisation of filming on location, for example for *Police Academy*, 1993) and distributes films (for example Soloviev's *Tender Age*). The company produced *Burnt by the Sun*, finding financial support from businesses in Nizhny Novgorod, where Mikhalkov had befriended Ivan Skliarov, a supporter of Boris Nemtsov.[7] TriTe is a successful, solid company with premises in the centre of Moscow, in Maly Kozikhinsky Lane.

Mikhalkov has maintained a principled stance in his public life, ranking personal loyalty above political expediency. So, for example, he resigned as chairman of the Russian Tennis Federation (a post he held from April 1990 to September 1995) when Evgeni Kafelnikov's personal coach Anatoli Lepeshin was appointed as captain of the Russian team rather than the candidate Vadim Borisov, whom he supported and favoured. Mikhalkov has also demonstrated firm support for a personal friend in the Pitirim affair. Pitirim was Metropolitan of Volokolamsk and Yurevsk, and in charge of the Church of the Resurrection in Briusov Lane (Moscow) – one of the few churches that remained open during the Soviet period and one which has traditionally attracted the artistic world. Mikhalkov supported Pitirim during the election of People's Deputies in the late 1980s, when Pitirim served as a deputy (1989–1991). In April 1992 Tatiana Mitkova, then presenter of the Second Channel's television news programme 'Vesti' ('News'), spoke in her programme of evidence that confirmed connections between Pitirim and the KGB. Mikhalkov, hosting the programme 'Perekrestok' ('Crossroads') on the First Channel (Ostankino), which was scheduled immediately after the programme 'Vesti', raised the question why the KGB lists of collaborators only disclosed the names of members of the intelligentsia and religious leaders, while no government officials and deputies were named. In fact, the release of the information was an attempt to discredit the Church, steered by the democrats, who had needed the Church to rise to power but who were now worried about its increasing influence in social and political life. 'Perekrestok' was removed from the schedule and Mikhalkov quit Ostankino television. In the aftermath of the affair Pitirim was replaced as Metropolitan of Volokolamsk and Yurevsk in 1994. Mikhalkov's solidarity with Pitirim in those years serves not only as an example of his reliability as a friend, no matter what the politics, but also as evidence of his commitment to the Church.

Mikhalkov is also actively involved with the Russian Culture Foundation, which was established in 1986 and has 52 regional branches. It is supported by UNESCO and organises a variety of cultural events. In the late 1980s it was headed by the academician Dmitri Likhachev, who, together with Raisa Gorbacheva, organised a number of activities for the foundation. In January 1992 Mikhalkov, who had in 1987 donated his honorarium for the theatre production of *Mechanical Piano* to the Russian Culture Foundation,[8] joined the presidium. On 21 May 1993 he was elected president of the foundation, while Dmitri Likhachev remained honorary president. The foundation occupies a building in the centre of Moscow on Gogol Boulevard, right next to the Cathedral of Christ the Saviour. Shortly after Mikhalkov's election, on 18 February 1994, the building burnt down, and Mikhalkov raised money for its magnificent restoration through donations from companies (the sugar company Sucden, the Vneshtorg-Bank) and generous individuals. Under Mikhalkov's presidency the Russian Culture Foundation has organised exhibitions and gala evenings, book launches and concerts, and a variety of other cultural events. Some examples in recent years are: an evening dedicated to Tsar Nicholas II; an exhibition of photographs of the Nobel Prize-winning writer Ivan Bunin; an exhibition of the Georgian-born artist Zurab Tsereteli, the official artist for Moscow's government under Yuri Luzhkov;[9] a soirée to honour the Russian Nobel Prize recipients (2001); an evening devoted to the painter Vasili Surikov (Mikhalkov's great-grandfather on the maternal side); a concert by the viola player Yuri Bashmet to mark Russia's Independence Day (2001); a 15-volume edition of Pushkin's works in English (1999); the return of cultural heritage collections to Russia; the restoration of icons; the return of émigré archives to Russia (such as the papers of Ivan Bunin, 1870–1953, and Ivan Shmelev, 1873–1950, who both emigrated in the 1920s); and the organisation of a festival of Russian art in Cannes. The Russian Culture Foundation is also engaged in a number of youth contests in the arts, and actively supports the Orthodox Church and its publications.

Mikhalkov has been involved with a variety of parties and political organisations. Although his political allegiance seems to shift, he always supports a faction that maintains the status quo and, broadly speaking, represents an enlightened form of conservatism. His political career began as adviser in culture and international cultural links to Ivan Silayev, chairman of the Russian Federation's Council of Ministers (1990/91, when the Russian Federation – RSFSR – was still the major constituent republic of the Soviet Union). Later (1992–1993) he was unofficial adviser to Alexander Rutskoi,[10] and, as a personal friend, Mikhalkov proactively helped and hid Rutskoi's family during the attempted coup in October 1993, after which Rutskoi was arrested. During 1993 Mikhalkov endorsed the Citizens' Movement that was close to Rutskoi; later in the year there were rumours about Mikhalkov's candidacy for the Federal Council as deputy for the constituency of Nizhny Novgorod for the then Deputy Prime Minister Sergei Shakhrai's party 'Russian Unity and Consent'.[11] Mikhalkov moved swiftly away from the Citizens' Movement towards the party that backed the then Prime Minister Viktor Chernomyrdin's party 'Russia, Our Home' ('Nash Dom Rossiia');[12] in September 1994 he was the second name on the party's electoral list, and in December 1995 he was elected to a seat in the Duma, which he declined as he realised that he could not commit sufficient time to politics while working on his new film. Mikhalkov openly considered standing for the presidential elections in 1995 and in 2000. None of Mikhalkov's political endeavours represents an ideological position; rather, he sides with people who have helped him or who are influential, such as Chernomyrdin, who allocated a large sum from the state budget to the production of *The Barber of Siberia*. None of Mikhalkov's political favourites has had a long-lasting impact on politics, however powerful they all were.

Mikhalkov's meddling in the politics of cinema was also rather ill-fated. The Soviet Film-makers' Union had refused to elect Mikhalkov to the powerful chairmanship in 1986. The FU was the first of the creative unions to undergo significant transformation after the accession of Gorbachev. This change was instigated by Alexander Yakovlev, the chargé d'affaires for culture in the Central Committee, placed there in order to effect change in the cultural sector. During the fifth congress of the Soviet Film-makers' Union in 1986 Yakovlev nominated Elem Klimov for the chairmanship. Mikhalkov, who had warned against the loss of tradition and supported Sergei Bondarchuk, trying to protect the old guard of film-makers from being cast out and sidelined by the new chairman, was not elected. Eleven years later the FU faced a dismal situation: the veterans' home at Krasnaya Pakhra was rotting away; the sanatoria in Matveyevo and Bolshevo were in need of repair; and the Cinema Centre (KinoTsentr) was the object of a legal dispute between the Russian FU and the Confederation of Former Soviet FUs (headed by Rustam Ibragimbekov). The Moscow Film Festival, traditionally presided over by the FU's chairman, no longer lived up to its status of an 'A' category festival – largely due to a boycott led by the Motion Picture Association of America to instigate a clampdown on video piracy, which had cost the American film industry huge sums of money; this had led to the absence of international stars at the festival. These tasks were addressed at the third congress of the Russian FU in December 1997. Mikhalkov offered neither solutions nor a programme, but promised to get to grips with the situation and solve issues step by step. He asked for a vote of trust, and he was elected chairman with an overwhelming majority of votes. He brought in a very effective team, including economists, lawyers and estate agents to manage the FU's affairs.

In his speech to the fourth FU plenary congress, held in grand style in the Kremlin Palace of Congresses in May 1998, Mikhalkov proposed the creation of an extra-budgetary fund to support the film industry, to be set up with fees collected from licensing video retail, which would be invested in the reconstruction of cinemas, the production of new films, and the renovation and maintenance of the FU's properties.[13] He suggested, indirectly, that the

FU should take over certain functions that were at the time carried out by Goskino, and unintentionally anticipated its merger with the Ministry of Culture. This coincided with the retirement of Goskino's chairman Armen Medvedev in 1998, when Mikhalkov tried, but failed, to place TriTe's producer Leonid Vereshchagin in the chair; instead, Armen Medvedev's deputy, the Petersburger Alexander Golutva, became head of Goskino.

Mikhalkov's speech also made perfectly clear what the task of a national Russian cinema should be: he criticised the preponderance of scenes of cruelty, violence and murder in contemporary Russian films and claimed that the representation of violence in film was not in proportion to reality. He argued strongly for the need to instil hope in the cinema audience, and dwelt on the need to create the myth of a Russian national hero in order to regain the spirit of patriotism that bonded the Soviet Union in the past, and that bonded the United States in the present.[14] He perceived the function of cinema as to perfect reality, to create a perfect future by transforming the here and now.

At the fifth FU congress in November 2001 Mikhalkov presented a positive result from his first period as chairman. After Goskino had been disbanded in May 2000, the Ministry of Culture had guaranteed a substantial budget for the Department of Cinema, now headed by Sergei Lazaruk (Golutva had moved on to Deputy Minister of Culture). By a resolution of the Ministry of Property (which arrived on the day of the congress) the estate of the Cinema Centre was transferred from the confederation to the Russian FU. The regional unions were subordinated to the Russian union. The FU's property in Krasnaya Pakhra had been sold and the profit was set to pay for the repairs and refurbishment of the houses of veterans in Bolshevo and Matveyevo. The FU's role in terms of its creative and legal support to its members remained vague and undefined, so the FU is clearly a much less powerful organisation than it was in Soviet times. Yet Mikhalkov has put his connections and power at the service of an institution primarily concerned with the care of veterans and pensioners, securing social benefits and the provision of care.

After his election to the chairmanship of the Film-makers' Union Mikhalkov became ex officio president of the (biennial) Moscow International Film Festival. In 1999 he moved the festival onto an annual basis, having secured consent from the then Prime Minister Stepanov and President Yeltsin. With his international renown as an Oscar winner Mikhalkov has been able to raise the level of the Moscow Film Festival significantly, after the festival's reputation had dropped to such an extent that even its status in the 'A' category had become questionable. While the competition programme of the first year (1999) was still rather weak, the standards increased with every year, as did the renown of the jury members. More and more internationally known film-makers entered their films into competition, including Krzysztof Zanussi,

Patrice Leconte, Bob Rafelson and the Taviani brothers. The juries were chaired by Theodor Angelopoulos, Margarethe von Trotta and Chingis Aitmatov. Mikhalkov also brought to Moscow an increasing number of world-class stars, including Jack Nicholson, Peta Wilson and Sean Penn (2001) and Jacqueline Bisset, Harvey Keitel and Holly Hunter (2002).

Private and Public Image

Mikhalkov maintains an excellent relationship with the media: he is always keen to be interviewed or photographed, and ready to appear on television. He is one of the few film-makers who is aware of the need to market his public image.

Mikhalkov was married first to Anastasia A. Vertinskaya (b. 1944), the daughter of the *estrada* singer Alexander Vertinsky and a well-known actress at the Moscow Arts Theatre; their marriage produced a son, Stepan (b. 1966), who makes music videos and is well established in the film business. Mikhalkov then married the model Tatiana E. Solovieva (b. 1947). They have three children: Anna (b. 1973), an actress and television presenter for the children's programme 'Good Night, Kids' [Spokoinoi nochi, malyshi]; Artem (b. 1975), a film director, who graduated from VGIK; and Nadezhda (Nadia, b. 1986), who has acted in several films but is still at school. Tatiana Mikhalkova knows very well how to present herself in the shadow of her husband; and the children Nadia, Anna and Artem frequently pose for the cameras of photo correspondents and film-makers.

In the post-Soviet period Mikhalkov has excelled at marketing not only his image but also his films. The film *Burnt by the Sun* was subjected to a stunning marketing campaign in Russia; at a time when the distribution network had almost collapsed, Mikhalkov travelled with the film and projection equipment through Russia to present the film to provincial audiences. Together with the distillery Kristall he launched the vodka brand 'KomDiv' ('Divisional Commander'), with his profile as Kotov on the bottle label. The publicity campaign around *The Barber* was carefully coordinated by a specially hired PR manager. Banners and posters were positioned all over central Moscow and a new brand of vodka, 'Russian Standard', was launched, as well as new perfume ranges, 'Cadet No. 1' and 'Cadet No. 3'. A shawl by Hermès, designed especially for the premiere, was offered to selected guests. Mikhalkov appeared for over a week on almost all television shows, and several channels screened retrospectives of his films. The premiere brought together Moscow's beau monde in the Kremlin Palace of Congresses, specially fitted with a Dolby Stereo Surround system and a new projection screen for this purpose. The publicity campaign connected Mikhalkov's role in the film to his political programme, giving rise to speculation about his candidature during the presidential elections scheduled for 2000, which in turn benefited the promotional campaign for the film. The media hype drove most Russian journalists – unaccustomed to such a PR campaign for a Russian product – to review the film in negative terms, while Russian audiences loved the film. Mikhalkov connected his role in the film as the loved tsar to his potential as presidential candidate. He no longer separated film from reality, film-making from politics, myth from history. 'What is a President? It is a person who is loved. [...] The task of a President is to create an atmosphere in the country, to direct the atmosphere of the nation.'[15]

Mikhalkov has cast himself in the role of a charismatic leader, a father-figure for his family, his actors and film crew, and his audiences. His role is enhanced by the parts that he chooses for himself in his own films, where he appears as a political and moral leader of the nation.

2. Dreams of a Better Life: 1963–1975

Nikita Sergeyevich Mikhalkov entered the arena of film-making at the time when a man who shared his Christian name and patronymic ruled the country: Nikita Sergeyevich Khrushchev. By 1963 the Thaw was drawing towards a close, but the arts still benefited from a certain degree of liberalism. After Khrushchev's 'secret speech' at the 20th Party Congress, in which he disclosed the crimes of the Stalin era, a period of liberalisation set in both in political and cultural terms. The Thaw had a number of positive effects on cultural life: the publication of works that were critical of Soviet society, such as the appearance in 1962 of Alexander Solzhenitsyn's *A Day in the Life of Ivan Denisovich*, about life in a prison camp; the opening of new theatres, such as the Sovremennik and Taganka Theatres; the move away from the glorification of collective Soviet heroism towards an individual heroism in films such as Mikhail Kalatozov's *The Cranes are Flying* [Letiat zhuravli, 1957], or Grigori Chukhrai's *Ballad of a Soldier* [Ballada o soldate, 1959]; the opening of modern art exhibitions, such as the Picasso exhibition of 1956 or the scandalous Manege exhibition of 1962, when Khrushchev labelled the abstract paintings in the exhibition as 'shit' and their painters 'sodomites'; the opening of artistic cafés in 1961; and the celebration of the International Youth Festival in Moscow in 1957. However, the Thaw also had a reverse side, which reflected the struggle within the Party between hard liners and reformers; the crushing of the reformist uprising in Hungary in 1956, the refusal to let Boris Pasternak accept the Nobel Prize in 1958 for his novel *Doctor Zhivago*, which had been published in Italy, and the arrest of the poet Joseph Brodsky in 1964 for 'parasitism' (not having a job) are examples of the hardline communists gaining the upper hand. The tension between the two factions in the Central Committee of the Communist Party climaxed with the removal of Khrushchev from office in October 1964. The period which followed under Brezhnev's leadership is commonly called the period of 'stagnation', as it consolidates communist rule through pragmatic policies rather than opening an ideological debate about the adaptation of communism to contemporary society. The period is further characterised by a much more aggressive policy, manifest in internal politics in the arrest of Andrei Siniavsky and Yuli Daniel in 1966 for publishing abroad under the pseudonyms of Abram Terts and Nikolai Arzhak, and in foreign politics in the intervention in Czechoslovakia in 1968. This increased suppression of opposition led to the emergence of a dissident movement that began formally with a letter protesting against Soviet foreign policy in 1967, signed by a number of members of the Soviet Writers' Union.

In these last years of the Thaw Mikhalkov began a course in acting at the Vakhtangov Theatre's Shchukin School.[1] Throughout his career Mikhalkov has appeared in over 30 films, and his popularity as an actor preceded that as a director. Mikhalkov had begun his acting career as a teenager with two minor roles, in Konstantin Voinov's *The Sun Shines for All* [1959], about a soldier returning from the war, losing his eyesight and his wife but finding fulfilment in teaching, and in Vasili Ordynsky's *Clouds over Borsk* [1960], about a Komsomol girl drawn to a sect. He also played the main part of Vadim in Genrikh Oganisian's *The Adventures of Krosh* [1961], based on a story by Anatoli Rybakov about a school class enjoying vacation work in a car factory, with the exception of the technically uninterested Sergei Krasheninnikov (Krosh), who becomes sidelined from the rest of the boys, until a car is stolen and he engages in the detective work.

Then Mikhalkov was cast for the part that would bring him huge popularity: Kolka in *I Walk Around Moscow* [1963] by Georgi Daneliya, a young film-maker of Georgian descent who would become a very popular figure in the 1970s.[2] Kolka (the short form of Nikolai) is a young metro construction worker, who makes the acquaintance of a visitor, the technical worker and writer Ermakov, on the metro on his way home. He accompanies the visitor into the capital and directs him to the address he seeks, and, when Ermakov returns without having found anyone at home, Kolka invites him to leave his bag at his home. Having worked the night shift, Kolka manages to sleep for an hour before his pal Sasha wakes him up. Sasha wants Kolka to help him get his draft into the army deferred by a few days so that he can marry first. With charm and a brilliant imagination Kolka manages to get the deferral for Sasha, but now Sasha doubts the commitment of his fiancée and almost calls off the wedding. The wedding goes ahead, but when the bride learns of Sasha's immediate departure she is upset. Kolka saves the situation by selflessly taking the blame and bringing the two sides together for their wedding night. Kolka accompanies Ermakov to the editor of the journal *Yunost*, where Ermakov's first story has been published. On the way they make the acquaintance of Alena, who works in a record shop. Kolka facilitates a happy reunion between Alena and Ermakov, before the latter leaves for his construction work in the provinces with a promise that Alena will visit. With Alena and Ermakov united, and Sasha and Sveta married, Kolka is a catalyst for meetings with happy endings. As a metro construction worker he is glorified as a builder of the new Moscow, while he remains alone: he is at one with the metro and the city, and this harmonious union is ultimately more stable (Ermakov departs, Sasha is drafted into the army) and long-lasting than personal relationships. The city of Moscow is what Kolka knows best: he guides a visitor in a taxi, shows Ermakov around, argues with a metro passenger about the quickest connection to Ermakov's destination. He knows his way around, both underground and over ground, and achieves his personal happiness in harmony with the city, the metro escalators and trains. The final image of the film represents this bond with Moscow, as Kolka leaves the 'University' metro station on an escalator, singing the title song (lyrics by Gennadi Shpalikov). Happiness lies in contributing to the great construction work of the metro, and it is this experience that Kolka will one day take with him when he sets out to explore the vastness of the Soviet land and find happiness there. Mikhalkov here

1. *I Walk Around Moscow*, Kolka (Nikita Mikhalkov) and Alena (Galina Polskikh)

played a role not dissimilar to his ambitions in real life: the popular son of the writer of the Soviet anthem became the 'king' of Moscow, who would later take his fame across the Soviet Union. Moreover, he represents a lifestyle rather than offering a psychological character portrayal; the figure of Kolka has no past, and no depth.[3] Kolka is a carefree contemporary child of the post-war period, who looks into the future rather than being crippled by the horrors of the war and the purges of the 1930s.

Mikhalkov acted in a number of films throughout the 1960s, including the main parts in Yuri Egorov's *Not the Luckiest Day* [1966], Daniil Khrabrovitsky's *Roll-Call* [1965] and Andrei Smirnov's *A Small Joke* [1966]. In 1969 he appeared in his elder brother's film adaptation of Ivan Turgenev's novel *A Nest of Gentlefolk* [1969], where he played Count Nelidov. The count features in an episode towards the end of the film, where he is accompanied by a group of gypsies. He attends the auction of a horse that he wants to purchase, but Lavretsky bids higher in an attempt to demonstrate his superiority and make up for his non-aristocratic background by showing his financial solidity, as opposed to the count's limited resources. In the manner and style of a vagabond aristocrat who drinks and gambles, who is full of love for life and surrounded by the bursting energy of the gypsies, not taking offence at Lavretsky's provocation, Mikhalkov's Nelidov anticipates the character of Paratov in Eldar Riazanov's *A Cruel Romance*, an adaptation of Ostrovsky's *Without a Dowry*, which is discussed later. Mikhalkov's early roles reveal his talent as a charmer, full of *joie de vivre*, embodying the optimism of the late Thaw period. It is this coincidence with the spirit of the time that made Mikhalkov such a popular actor at the very beginning of his career.

While still a student at the film school Mikhalkov made the film *Things* [1967] as part of his coursework. In this early film he demonstrates his ability to tell a story without words: a little girl wakes up in the morning and explores the leftovers of a party her parents held the previous evening. The eight-minute film begins and ends with a view of the outside world, moving from the warm inside through a window on to the snowy city. The camera moves around the room, halting occasionally on pictures, decorative objects, the window or the bed. The girl pulls a veil over her face and looks at the room through the veil. She squints at the pictures of her ancestors on the wall. Rapid montage makes the world around her move. She peers through a looking-glass at a cactus, and the camera moves with her, before looking on to the looking-glass and into a mirror. The camera experiences different views of the world together with the girl.

Mikhalkov refrains from dialogue and tells his story through objects: women's clothes on a chair, glasses, an ashtray hint at the leftovers of a party. There is very little non-diegetic music; instead, the girl plays with a tape recorder, hearing first music, then listening to a recorded conversation. She plays with the glasses on the table, tipping one over, and its contents trickle down the table onto the floor as she takes a glass and catches the drops under the table. Through objects, viewing devices and the playback of voices Mikhalkov allows the spectator to explore the world with the little girl while refraining from a narrative. Mikhalkov skilfully dwells on details and objects rather than the verbal plot. He manifests his interest in the contrast between inside and outside and in the panning over the landscape at beginning and end. The film also reveals his interest in viewing devices (looking-glass, mirror, window), which would continue to preoccupy Mikhalkov in his mature films.

A Quiet Day at the End of the War

This 38-minute-long film, shot in black and white, was completed in 1970 as Mikhalkov's diploma work upon graduation from VGIK. It was produced at Mosfilm's 'Time' ('Vremia') studio. The film begins and ends with a panning view of the territory, the Russian land near the Western border in its vastness. This panning shot had been introduced in *Things* and would remain a trademark for Mikhalkov as opening or final frame throughout most of his career. The opening shot is filmed through the lens of a telescopic rifle sight with a graticulate frame (a device that displays a cross to mark the target in the viewfinder), which reveal the open fields and a destroyed village in the distance. The shot underlines the information given by the intertitle: it is 1944, the end of the war on the Western front. The binoculars are held by a soldier, Andrei, who is standing on the rooftop of a ruined church. He spots some wooden cases that have been left in the fields. Despite his injured and bandaged leg he pulls the large wooden trunks across the field towards the church. His sergeant, Kolia, who is resting inside the destroyed building, warns him against tampering with these boxes and orders him to leave them where they were, as otherwise the enemy might come searching for them. The boxes contain paintings that were evacuated during the war to remote shelters in order to protect them; these 'hidden treasures' are now being collected by the retreating German army. The two trunks were left behind when the Germans were loading a truck, and the art-loving Andrei is eager to see the contents.

A car with two Russian soldiers (one male, one female) and two civilians (an older man and a young women) arrives. The woman is also in search of the paintings and wants to inspect the content of the trunks, so that they can be collected by the Russian army the next day. Andrei prevents the inspection, arguing that the woman has no documents and should get written permission to view and remove the paintings first. The injured sergeant Kolia takes the opportunity of catching a ride back to the garrison when the Kazakh woman soldier, Adalat, agrees to give up her place in the car and stay behind to await the collection of the pictures the next day.

Adalat eyes the landscape – and Andrei – through the binoculars. Andrei and Adalat make acquaintance: she is from Alma-Ata and married; he is from Vologda and has suffered a neck injury during the war. The film focuses on insignificant details rather than heroic feats: Adalat enquires about the light-bulb tattoo on Andrei's chest; through the binoculars she spots a scar on his neck. While Andrei wants to talk about himself and the past, Adalat does not. The two clearly respond differently to the horrors of the war they have witnessed. They settle in the peaceful idyll of the countryside. Andrei exhibits the paintings in the sun and moans about damage done to the glass and the frames. Adalat begins to dance in the room, then in the fields, before going for a swim in the river: she rejoices in the small pleasures of life. Andrei scares her by hiding and not answering her calls: he is much more immature than Adalat. As they return from the river, they spot several German soldiers in the church ruin, inspecting the pictures. Adalat asks Andrei not to shoot and wait for the Germans to leave. Yet Andrei makes a case for defending 'his' paintings, as though they were not objects but had a soul: he worries about art at a time when his life and that of a fellow soldier could be put at risk by a single wrong move.

The Germans start a brawl and damage a picture, prompting Andrei to fire a shot. A German soldier (played by Yuri Bogatyrev), mistakenly thinking that a can thrown in the sand by Andrei to lure out the enemy is a game of his fellow soldiers, is shot by Andrei when he peers out of the window. Andrei will kill the enemy as punishment, rather than in self-defence. The flames still flickering in the ruins flare up and Andrei, trying to rescue the pictures, is shot in the back. The last remaining German soldier runs away into the field as Adalat, who has been watching the scene, rises from her hiding position in the fields. With tears rolling down her cheeks she fires a shot in the direction of the German soldier. She returns to the church, packs the pictures into their boxes, and begins to ring the church bell for help and to draw attention to herself. In the dark, the headlights of a truck appear on the horizon: the Russians return to collect their soldiers and the art treasures.

The film establishes a number of features for Mikhalkov's future work, above all in terms of artistic collaboration. The two main actors are Natalia Arinbasarova[4] and Sergei Nikonenko.[5] The Kazakh-born Arinbasarova was Andrei Konchalovsky's first wife, Nikonenko a popular actor who would appear in episodes in Mikhalkov's later films. Other minor parts were played by actors such as Alexander Kaidanovsky, Yuri Bogatyrev and Alexander Porokhovshchikov,[6] who would feature in Mikhalkov's later films. Mikhalkov wrote the script with Rustam Ibragimbekov, and would again write scripts with him in the 1990s; he began the collaboration with the composer Eduard Artemiev that would continue in his later works; finally, the art direction of Alexander Adabashian would lay the foundation for more than a decade of joint work with him as designer, and later as scriptwriter.

A Quiet Day is shot in an interesting manner: Mikhalkov uses the telescopic rifle sight as a viewing device. The vast and open landscape of Russia is mechanically viewed and searched for danger rather than appreciated for its beauty in the days immediately after the war. The focus on the church as a shelter for the soldiers is an interesting choice of location in that it reflects, on the one hand, the religious symbolism of the church. On the other hand, by using the church as a place of physical (rather than spiritual) shelter and as refuge for art treasures, the church is turned into a museum, which echoes the fate of many churches after Stalin's campaign of church destruction and conversion in the 1930s.

The plot raises a number of issues without, however, offering a clear standpoint of the director, as would be characteristic of Mikhalkov's later work. He alludes to the theme of the common goal that Soviet people have fought for in the war: a common goal uniting North (Andrei) and South (Adalat), European Russia and Central Asia, and bringing together the Soviet people in their variety of national backgrounds. However, whether Andrei's and Adalat's actions are different because of ethnic and national background or because of their gender remains unexplored. Mikhalkov merely raises the issue of Russia's vast expanse, and her allegiance both to Europe and Asia – an issue much discussed in the debate on 'Eurasianism', which sees Russia's unique geographical position between two continents as a mission to form a bridge between Western and Eastern cultures. This theme will become important in Mikhalkov's later films.

Neither of the characters is given a full-blown psychological portrayal. Their past is told through details and gestures rather than through flashbacks: Andrei's scar alludes to his feats in the war, as does the injury. He has fought in the war, while the tattoo underpins his immaturity and alludes to his Party commitment: Lenin's appeal to electrify the country led to a slogan about Lenin's (Ilyich's – he was Vladimir Ilyich Lenin) light bulb, the *lampochka Il'icha*. Adalat's dance and bathing reflect her love for life, and cast her into a stereotypical female role as she lacks political commitment. Information is sketchy and incoherent, and the actors have to bring out their past through their actions in the present.

Andrei is immature: he fools around at a time when it is not safe to do so, and is reprimanded for this both by Adalat verbally (after hiding from her) and by his sergeant (who leaves him after he has pulled in the boxes). Andrei acts on the spur of the moment, without thinking of the consequences. He places the paintings higher on his scale of responsibility than protecting himself and another fellow soldier, putting his and her life at risk by shooting at the Germans. Moreover, the killing of the Germans is entirely unnecessary, and they are portrayed not as the enemy but as people who are roaming the countryside at the end of the war, themselves unaware of any danger that might be lurking. In fact, the German soldier played by Bogatyrev is as naïve as Andrei when he assumes that a comrade is playing a game, tossing a can into the sand. The end of war could have brought quietude, but it is through underestimating the danger that the 'quiet day' brings death to the Germans and to Andrei. Effectively, they die for no values and no reason. The dream of peace is shattered before it even has begun.

Mikhalkov never condemns Andrei's concern and love for the pictures, though. Andrei treats the pictures as his friends: there is a subtle allusion that Andrei has nobody left (he has lost his brother during the war), and 'adopts' the paintings. In this sense, Andrei is a sad boy, and may be forgiven his lack of apprehension of the situation, unforgivable as it may be for the soldier Andrei. Mikhalkov's concept of art as something sacred, yet containing danger, emerges in this film in a rudimentary form. The concept itself would be developed in later films. *A Quiet Day* is an accomplished film, both for its cinematic achievements and for the ambiguity that the director reserves for himself with regard to his main characters. Mikhalkov alludes to the conflict between personal and political that dominates a number of his films, without here resolving it in favour of one or the other. In Mikhalkov's first full-length feature film his political commitment would be clear, while some of the fragmentation of the narrative, by skipping events and focusing on the consequences rather than the facts, remains visible. The use of flashback to fill in on psychological background would become more prominent and obtrusive.

After his debut as a director Mikhalkov continued to act both in his own films and those made by his colleagues. One of his key roles in this period is in Sergei Soloviev's *The Stationmaster* [1972], based on one of Pushkin's *Tales of Belkin*, in the role of Captain Minsky, who stops at a station to change his horses. Minsky is so impressed with the stationmaster's daughter Dunia that he pretends to be ill and eventually elopes with Dunia to St Petersburg. The heartbroken stationmaster tries to visit Dunia, but is denied entrance into Minsky's house. When Dunia finally returns for a visit to her father's home with her children, it is too late: he has died. Soloviev employs three narrative voices: that of Belkin for his first visit to the station; that of the stationmaster telling Belkin about Dunia's elopement on his second visit; and, finally, the voice of the new stationmaster's son, who briefs Belkin about the most recent events. Mikhalkov plays the part of Minsky, a dashing Petersburg captain, who does not elicit a single word from Dunia, but who nevertheless takes control over her emotionally. Mikhalkov's Minsky always gets what he wants: he schemes, in order to stay longer, by pretending to be ill and bribing the doctor. In maturity Mikhalkov's roles change: he is no longer the naïve and light-hearted boy Kolka but a man who manipulates and plots, who does not mean to harm anyone, who never thinks of others but only of his own overall scheme – like a film director controlling his actors and the intrigue.

At Home Among Strangers, a Stranger at Home

By the time Mikhalkov embarked on his debut as a film-maker the cultural and political situation in the country had reached the depths of stagnation. In cinema the genre of comedy had taken top place in popularity, offering a comic relief to the dullness and gloom of everyday life after the 50th anniversary of the Revolution in 1967 and the 50th anniversary of the Soviet state in 1972. In the interim between these jubilees, artistic censorship saw an unprecedented rise in the number of theatre productions, literary works and films banned, refused and shelved. In 1967 Andrei Konchalovsky's *Asya's Happiness* was banned because of its open and honest portrayal of country life, and because it failed to offer a positive statement on the Soviet family and promulgated instead the role of single parents (Asya rejects the father of her child as husband, as he is an alcoholic, and prefers to raise her child alone). In a similar vein the production of *Fedor Kuzkin* (adapted from a novel by Boris Mozhayev) was banned at the Taganka Theatre in 1968 for failing to show life in the countryside in a positive light. It is curious to note that both the film and the production were shown to collective farm workers in order to pass judgement on their suitability and ideological correctness. Kira Muratova's film *Brief Encounters* [Korotkie vstrechi, 1967] was also banned for showing the vagrant life of a geologist, unable to settle and lead a 'normal' Soviet family life. In this period of repression, clampdown and a stifling cultural climate Mikhalkov turned to Soviet history, reminding us of the values of the Revolution while choosing the genre of an adventure film, which ranked among the most popular genres in Russian cinema.

At Home Among Strangers [1974] explores the events of the Civil War in the popular genre of an adventure film, with elements of a detective thriller and a Western with chases on horseback and fist fights. The film tells of the trust that the Cheka[7] collective places in Egor Shilov (played by the tall, blond and blue-eyed Yuri Bogatyrev) to accompany a train with gold to the capital, where money is needed to purchase grain from abroad for the starving population. The train is robbed, and Egor takes it upon himself to prove that he was wronged and to retrieve the gold in a solitary fight against bandits and deserters. Although he acts alone, he is guided by the spirit of the collective (flashbacks recall again and again the happy past with his comrades), and by the desire to achieve the improvement of society. He supports the people, believing in the goals of socialism and its capacity to re-educate even thieves. The film focuses on the integrity and high moral values that Egor holds and inspires in others, rather than on the politics of socialism. As the critic Yuri Khaniutin has argued, 'They live like children, frankly, although they are capable of playing a clever game with the enemy; they are like fairy-tale heroes, acting according to the law of natural justice and believing in its triumph'.[8] As such, the film establishes the personal motivation for political expediency as crucial for political success, a feature also seen in *Quiet Day*, where personal values and the duty to the country are mixed up.

The film is set in the period immediately after the Revolution, when the Bolsheviks had taken power in November 1917. The former bourgeoisie vehemently opposed communist rule and formed the so-called 'White' army, which began to fight the 'Red' Bolshevik forces in an attempt to defy the new leadership. The ensuing Civil War raged from the Revolution until 1921, leaving the Red Army victorious and the country devastated. The war ravaged the countryside, depriving cities of supplies in the absence of farming and transportation. It is against this backdrop – the hardship of the years immediately following the Revolution – that Mikhalkov sets his first full-length feature film.

The film begins with a black and white sequence of a rider in the fields, establishing immediately one of Mikhalkov's favourite themes: the fields, woods and rivers of Russia, which are endowed with the same qualities in both Eastern and Western Russia. The shots continue with scenes of the laughter and amusement of a group of young men and a girl, carefree in their activities, rolling in the fields like boys playing 'sacks on the mill' (*kucha mala*, a game where three or more people lie on top of each other and toboggan down a hill). Jointly, they push an old carriage down a slope: the old order is being pushed down the hill, while a new means of transport takes over from there on, both historically and diegetically (in the film narrative): the train. Indirectly, Mikhalkov comments on the social change as well as on the industrialisation of the country, and he first uses here his favourite trope of a transport unit – a car, a train, a bicycle, a dirigible – that harbours an entire value system cocooned in a reality that adheres to another value system. This black and white flashback is inserted at several points during the film, offering a moment of recollection of a happy memory for the protagonist Egor Shilov and his comrades when they returned from the First World War (1914–1918). Now they are fighting in the Civil War (1918–1921) on the side of the Bolsheviks. Their camaraderie and trust in each other has remained unchanged, but the duties are grim and allow no space or time for distraction, as shown in the black and white scenes. Moreover it is only this scene that contains a female presence. The music, a song about dreams ('The Ballad of the Ship'),[9] underpins the theme of the hard work required to turn dreams into reality – a theme that would become a preoccupation in the Stalinist culture of the 1930s, as echoed in the slogan 'We turn the fairy tale into reality'. Both this song and the title song of *I Walk Around Moscow* present the image of a boat, embodying the free and adventurous future that comes as a reward for hard work.

The film then proceeds to an interior space: in one room an accountant is checking details as the nervous Sarychev thrusts a newspaper at the clock to stop it chiming, reminding him of the time spent waiting for orders to act. The atmosphere of impatience is further underlined by a close-up of a fly on a mirror, which provokes, when buzzing through the room, another nervous outbreak from Zabelin, also bored with the inactivity. The Revolutionaries are bursting with energy and impatient to be called to action. Yet, for the moment, their energy is stifled by the interior space of the room. From the stasis of the office setting the camera moves to the ticker band that is stretched across the screen. Dzerzhinsky's telegram asking for gold reserves to be sent to Moscow in order to alleviate the famine in the capital in the aftermath of the Civil War brings movement into the headquarters.

> To all Party District Committees and their heads: thousands of dying people need your help. The League of Nations has refused to support the starving Russian population. Bread only for gold. I order: speed up the dispatch to Moscow of gold and valuables confiscated from the bourgeoisie. Cheka Chairman Dzerzhinsky.

Together with three other Chekists Egor Shilov is sent to oversee the transport. He is chosen although his brother Fedor fought on the side of the Whites and Egor has never denounced him to the Bolsheviks. Egor receives a vote of confidence, and thus has a double obligation to do his job well. His manner is playful and jocular: after receiving his orders he opens the window and sings a song, underlining his vagrant, freedom-loving nature. He seems to have changed little since the end of the war seen in the flashback, while the other four men have grown serious and important: army commander Zabelin, committee chairman Sarychev, district chairman Kungurov, and Lipiagin.

In the meantime the invidiously fat and slimy railway pointsman Vaniukin (his name suggests 'smelly' – from *voniat'* [to smell], *voniushchii* [smelly]), played by the small and stout Alexander Kaliagin,[10] is bribed: danger is looming. This is reinforced in the next scene, when a body – believed to be Shilov's – with a disfigured face is found. While Shilov's comrades are saddened by the loss of a friend, enhanced both by melancholic music and a sequence of black and white flashbacks to the happy past, they prepare for the immediate departure of the gold.

In the vicinity of the switch-stand five counter-Revolutionaries and bandits (Turchin, Lemke, Lebedev, Solodovnikov and Belenky) are preparing for a train robbery. With the assistance of Vaniukin fiddling the points they jump onto the roof of the train, disconnect the last carriage and sidetrack it towards a destroyed bridge. They seize the gold and – having seen the separated carriage tumble down an abyss into a river – they run back to the train, which is waiting by a false signal. Once on the train, the four (Solodovnikov has been killed) continue the journey. The short cuts of the shots showing the train in the open field with the men chasing it on horseback and hijacking it by climbing onto the roof, and the music for this sequence, both reveal Mikhalkov's endorsement of elements of the Western. Similarly, the costumes are evocative of American Westerns.

Once the counter-Revolutionaries have hijacked the train, another robbery ensues: the Cossack captain (*esaul*) Brylov, played by Mikhalkov, boss of a gang of gypsies and bandits, stops the train. Brylov walks on the tracks with a great presence, his horse being led by a small boy. In this way he brings the train to a halt. Brylov is a gentleman bandit, protecting a girl on the train from the sexual advances of one of the gypsies. During this second robbery two

2. *At Home Among Strangers*, Brylov (Nikita Mikhalkov)

more of the counter-Revolutionaries, Turchin and Lebedev, are killed, before Lemke liquidates Belenky in the hope of seizing the gold and keeping it for himself. Lemke (portrayed with devious features by Alexander Kaidanovsky) follows Brylov to the gypsy camp, since he is certain that the gold – of which Brylov is unaware – must be in the sacks with the loot. At headquarters, in the meantime, Sarychev (played by the reflective Solonitsyn[11]) tries to keep calm when he learns of the train robbery and Shilov's disappearance. Before long Shilov returns, after having been drugged and detained by the counter-Revolutionaries for three days. In the white room of his quarters he tries to remember what happened, but all he sees are flashes of white and black. Zabelin, agitated and hot-headed like the film hero Chapayev, in a brilliant performance by Sergei Shakurov, accuses Shilov all too easily, yet he realises Shilov's despair when the latter smashes a window with his fist, as if he could obtain clarity by removing the opaque veil of the glass.[12] Rather as in *Things*, Mikhalkov uses imagery rather than words to express the emotions that underlie the conversation between the men, who are fighting for the same goal but see their trust in each other waning. The juxtaposition of inside and outside, and the acts of deliberate physical injury to ease the emotional tension (standing in the rain, breaking the window), underline the duplicity of feelings that rules these characters.

Finally, Shilov remembers Vaniukin's face. Shilov escapes as he is taken to prison for treason, and finds and interrogates Vaniukin, who leads him to Brylov. Events now happen at great speed: Shilov sends Vaniukin to the headquarters to confess; Vaniukin admits that he has drugged Shilov; Vaniukin is forced to act as bait to catch the thief of the gold. Zabelin leaves with the cavalry to chase Brylov and retrieve the gold, accompanied by the waltz 'Farewell to the Slavianka' ('Proshchanie Slavianki') that traditionally accompanies all departures of the Russian military. Vaniukin is reported killed in his cell by a left-hander: there must be a spy in the Cheka headquarters. Suspicion reigns as Sarychev tests even Kungurov's reaction. Having used elements of the Western for the robbery scenes, Mikhalkov now builds on elements of the detective story: he raises suspense by the question mark over the unknown identity of the spy.

Shilov meets the native Asian boy Kadyrkul (a skilful performance by Konstantin Raikin), who leads him to the gold. When Kadyrkul tries to kill Shilov and run away with the gold, Shilov actually saves Kadyrkul's life when the non-swimmer falls into the water; Shilov wins Kadyrkul's absolute trust and devotion. Honesty and model behaviour make Shilov a winner all the time, not just once. Shilov takes Lemke hostage (Lemke knows the spy in the Cheka), but Brylov has stolen the gold. Another true Western-style chase follows: Shilov and Kadyrkul chase Brylov, floating down the wild mountain river to catch up with him. In the chase Kadyrkul is killed; Lemke tries to join up with Brylov, who shoots at him; Shilov kills Brylov, and finally recaptures the gold, taking Lemke hostage. In line with the Soviet ethos of the 1920s the Russian Revolutionary plays the role of a father figure for a man (almost his own age) from an ethnic minority, enhancing the Revolutionaries' moral superiority and leadership capacity.

Lemke tries to convince Shilov to share the gold with him and run across the border to Mongolia. Yet Shilov resists temptation and provocation alike; instead, in a long sequence, he carries the injured enemy through the woods, hoping to take him to headquarters in order to extract from him the name of the spy. As Zabelin rides with his cavalry through the steppe, followed by a black car in which Sarychev, who has accepted responsibility for the unsuccessful mission, is travelling, Shilov emerges on the horizon. Unable to utter a single sound after the exhaustion of carrying Lemke through the forest, Shilov is sighted immediately and embraced by his brothers-in-arms. The finale brings home the spirit of the Revolution, which forges friendships that last for ever, based on honesty and trust in the comrades of the Revolution. The theme of the brotherhood, the alliance of people on an equal footing, triumphs over the Cossack gang led by Brylov: among comrades no leadership is needed. Mikhalkov stresses that the ideal must be right, but that the personal commitment in which the fight for this ideal is anchored is most important. He thus defines the relationship between personal and political as reciprocal.

The plot of the film is complex and often confusing, especially when events are not always shown as explicitly as they are contained in the scenario. Mikhalkov focuses on themes rather than events, often leaving out the facts and showing reactions only, as if making a detective story in which the spectator knows less (or no more) than the investigator. Yet he applies this technique to the genre of an adventure movie, where it would help to define the opposing sides in the fight. In the style of the Western, Mikhalkov relies on speed, not explanation. Similarly, his heroes are not psychologically portrayed; instead they are types – revolutionaries, robbers, traitors. Genre duplicity serves the Western, but not so much the adventure genre.

It is interesting to note here the break in character in order to create a type: Shilov breaks the code of the Revolutionary when he flees, taking a risk that not only involves his life and honour but also puts at risk those comrades who have vouched for him.[13] For Shilov, the aim justifies the means used to achieve it; his action is justified by his character, and these characteristics are guaranteed as he is not an individual but a type: he will not change his attributes. He is a winner, a righteous Revolutionary. The Revolution thus depends on the combination of characters and the dynamic within a group: '… the key to the solution of the whole mix-up lies in the character of those involved'.[14] History, then, is a product of coincidences, while character types execute a function within the historical plot.

Reliability is shown as a stable, permanent trait of character: even Brylov believes Shilov more than he trusts the traitor Lemke regarding the loot. Lemke is a traitor and remains a traitor. There is, thus, no room for development; characters are types. Zabelin is a perfect agitator, a choleric, but an ideal performer for his soldiers, inspiring in them the right ideals before taking them to fight. The film's moral message is underlined by the dramatic music in crucial scenes, and a romantic, melodramatic tune for the flashbacks.

The rough montage of the film, cutting from close-ups to longer and medium shots without any consistency in their use, is complemented by often unmotivated shifts between black and white and colour. The movement of the camera is often such that the spectator is deprived of an overview, unable to recognise individual faces. The camera moves jerkily from close-ups of faces to long shots of the room, returning to close-ups of the clock, the fly on the window, the bin. The warm interior light is contrasted with the cold light outside, often flooding through the windows and creating such a stark opposing light that it blinds the camera. Due to the frequent changes between close, long and medium shots the image often appears blurred. Moreover, the camera follows the fast movement of characters, almost like a hand-held device. The impression of chaos and hurry created through the camerawork of Pavel Lebeshev in the action scenes is contrasted with moments of reflection and quietude. Mikhalkov makes subtle use of flashbacks: the flashback in black and white leads to a happy past. But there are also shots such as the murder of the traitor Nikodimov, which is filmed in a red tint; the murder of Vaniukin, shown through a series of black and white photos that give the event a documentary touch; and the robbery of the train, tinted in blue. Mikhalkov deploys a range of cinematic devices of colouring with filters to set apart and highlight events with a documentary character, endowing myth with authentic qualities.

> We are so attracted by the rhythm and the logic of the genre, so angry at the boldness of the mischief, that we probably only notice at a second viewing how the actors sometimes fail to reach a high note and lapse into rhetoric, how the subject-matter occasionally becomes incoherent, how objects accidentally appear in the frame. This film counts on love at first sight.[15]

Although the material aim is the retrieval of the gold, the most important theme is the trust in the collective, the 'brotherhood'. Lemke has no friend, nobody to rely on; he is lonely, and this is almost enough punishment, especially in the final scene, when Shilov is embraced by his comrades while Lemke is almost forgotten in the fields. The gold is recaptured, Brylov shot, the traitor revealed. In the final scene, the image of the old order represented by the carriage that featured in the black and white flashbacks becomes coloured: the past has caught up with the present, and the new order has won.

Ultimately, the opposition in the film is simple: it lies between Lemke and Shilov, between personal, material gain and selfless action for the community. The Cheka has to fight on several fronts (the counter-Revolutionaries led by Turchin, Brylov and his gang, the traitors Vaniukin and Nikodimov): their opposition is fragmented. It is this fragmentation of the enemy that underscores the unity of the Revolutionaries, and it is the spirit of acting in unity that makes the Revolutionaries triumph in the end. Shilov's greatest joy lies not in handing over the captured enemy, or in presenting the gold, but in falling back into the arms of his 'family', his best friends Zabelin, Kungurov and Sarychev. They may be accountable to the representative from Moscow; but ultimately they gaze at their 'father', Lenin, for guidance. When in doubt, alone in Shilov's flat after the 'murder', Sarychev stares at Lenin's portrait on the wall, seeking to elucidate the events and find an answer. The answer lies in trust – in his friends and in the cause – and this trust is confirmed by the return of Shilov with the gold. Mikhalkov aims not at an accurate version of events but at a popularisation and heroisation of the Revolution, at the creation of a myth. Mikhalkov's film is based on myth, not fact.

> The film does not resurrect with historical accuracy the atmosphere of the time, but recreates it afresh. Mikhalkov does not aim to tell the spectator 'this is how it was', but 'this is how it could have been, because this is what should have happened'. [...] The director aims to return to the screen our romantic hero. A hero gripped by personal passions about general and popular issues.[16]

Mikhalkov presents in true socialist spirit history 'as it should have been', while at the same time adapting this view to the popular genre of a Western with the suspense elements of an adventure film. Herein lies the film's success with both the masses and the officials. The film is also an early indication of Mikhalkov's approach to the past: he bases his work not on the historical facts but on a myth, creating an artistic and fictional version that is rooted not in a primary but in a secondary source, thus blurring the historical perspective. Mikhalkov deliberately creates a historical myth, longing for the brotherhood and the spirit of the time rather than returning to the period of the Civil War. Svetlana Boym makes a useful distinction between ironic and Utopian nostalgia, one dwelling on longing for, the other on rebuilding, the past. In her definition, *At Home Among Strangers* contains ironic, reflective nostalgia that emphasises the process of longing rather than the target of nostalgic feeling.[17]

Director of photography (DoP) Pavel Lebeshev's camera does not have much chance of panning on the countryside after the opening sequence and before the finale. Instead, the camera follows the chases of the Revolutionaries and counter-Revolutionaries in true Western style. However, Lebeshev offers numerous shots of the vast landscape when filming the train and the cavalry riding through the steppe. He also chooses a fine location for the river chase, with a mountain river gushing along its bed, hidden in an abyss without any connecting bridges: both the train bridge and the bridge on which Brylov tries to cross the border have been destroyed. Although the open steppe is an important setting, it is here not yet endowed with the qualities of the Russian homeland that would appear in Mikhalkov's later work.

Mikhalkov's debut film made a huge impact on the cinematic community, and was praised by the critics at the time as a film that struck a fine balance between popular cinema and heroism for the Soviet Union. It was shown at the International Film Festival in Delhi in 1975, where it received a special mention. With an overall audience of 23 million in the first year of its Soviet release, the film ranked among the top 20 films of the season.

Slave of Love

The permanence and ultimate superiority of the ideals of the Revolution also dominated Mikhalkov's second film, *Slave of Love*. The film is set in 1918, when many supporters of the Whites and former members of the bourgeoisie had moved to Southern Russia. The Civil War, with its fighting between Reds and Whites, was taking place on several fronts, but the capital – Moscow – was firmly held by the Reds. The history of the making of *Slave of Love* is a complex issue, imbued with scandals. In 1974 Mosfilm halted the production of the film *Unexpected Joys* [Nechaiannye radosti], directed by Rustam Khamdamov and based on a scenario by Friedrich Gorenstein and Andrei Konchalovsky. The film was stopped largely because of Khamdamov's inability to edit the film and his unwillingness to stick to the script. When Mosfilm stopped production, most of the film had been shot but not edited. In order not to write off a project that had already incurred expenditure, Mikhalkov was invited to look at the material and the script with a view to making his own film under the umbrella of the existing project. As the film was made in an experimental unit, the ticket sales had to pay for part of the production cost (the film was not wholly state-financed). Mikhalkov rewrote the script with Alexander Adabashian and started a new film. Despite the fact that the material filmed by Khamdamov was largely destroyed (only 20 minutes have survived), there is evidence of some influence. Khamdamov's designs for hats and costumes, and the loft-style building covered with a glass roof, decorated with palms and rattan furniture, which formed the film studio were all largely taken over for Mikhalkov's film. The casting of Elena Solovei, an actress of great sentimentality and spiritual elegance, was determined by the original cast list of *Unexpected Joys*.

Khamdamov's *Unexpected Joys* dealt with the silent film star Vera (Faith) and her sister Nadezhda (Hope), embroiled in the search for the carpet 'Shakh' (Shah), which – according to legend – has the power to halt the Revolution. The Bolshevik Potapov hides among the film crew and travels with them to Yalta. The film's director, Ardynin, gambles and wins the carpet; later he dies in a brawl. Ultimately, Russia is not saved from the Revolution: the legend turned out to be a false belief, and Vera dies. The sequence of Vera's death is among those re-shot for a film-within-a-film inset in Khamdamov's *Anna Karamazoff* [1991], which also concerns two actresses who buy the powerful, magic carpet from a man from Bukhara. Vera runs away, and gets her foot stuck between rails; rescue from a Cossack is not far away, but here the film ends, and it is never clear whether she survives or not. This open ending parallels the final scene in *Slave of Love*, where Olga travels on the tram into the distance, into an unknown future. If in Khamdamov's film the heroine sided with the Whites, in Mikhalkov's she would side with the Reds. The ethos of Khamdamov's film is anti-Revolutionary, while Mikhalkov's is pro.

While Mikhalkov's Olga is concerned only with her stardom and lives in a world apart, Khamdamov's Vera understands what is going on around her and takes a clear position against the Revolutionaries. In Mikhalkov's script the story with the carpet is removed, as is anything referring to fate or myth. The theme of the film within the film remains intact, as well as the storyline of the Revolutionaries and the Whites, and the hiding of a Revolutionary among the film crew. Apart from these isolated influences, Mikhalkov made an entirely different film. *Slave of Love* is about the chain of events that lead the silent film star Olga Voznesenskaya to support the Revolution and find a meaning in life.

Slave of Love opens with a pianist accompanying the screening of a silent film, 'Slave of Love', starring Olga Voznesenskaya. The film (within the film) shows a blind noblewoman (the diegetic actress Olga) playing a violin in a park, while her husband (the diegetic actor Ivan Maksakov) flirts with a young servant girl on the adjacent bench and tries to seduce her. The screening is interrupted by the intrusion of the Whites, led by Captain Fedotov. A man is arrested and led out of the auditorium, although he asserts that this is all a mix-up and that he is just a factory worker from the neighbouring town of Vinnitsa. He is beaten up and smashed into a window containing a poster for Voznesenskaya's new film. The frivolity of film is immediately contrasted with the harsh reality of life. The theme of film and reality is extended to the juxtaposition of private and public life. A bourgeois lifestyle is portrayed on film, and the film crew creates a domestic and bourgeois atmosphere in the studio. This is juxtaposed to the reality on the documentary film, the intrusion of the army into the screening and into the making of the film,

3. *Slave of Love*, Voznesenskaya (Elena Solovei)

which gradually forces the film crew out of their 'home' and removes fiction to replace it with reality (the takeover of the studio by the Bolsheviks).

Olga is modelled on the silent film star Vera Kholodnaya (real name Levchenko, 1893–1919), who had starred in early Russian films and was one of the most popular actresses of early Russian cinema, dying prematurely of influenza at the age of 26. Mikhalkov makes ironic comments on the antics of the film crew, who escape Moscow, struck by Civil War and under Bolshevik rule, and who take refuge in a town run by the Whites. The preoccupation with filming itself is seen as frivolous, unless it concerns capturing on film the injustice of the Whites. The film crew is mocked: the director Alexander Kaliagin is concerned with his obesity; the producer Savva Yuzhakov is preoccupied with the arrival of film stock (impossible to obtain after the nationalisation of the film industry and before the Treaty of Rapallo); the scriptwriter Veniamin Konstantinovich has a writing block; the actress Olga is concerned only with her image on screen. The film in production concerns the life of the past: the seduction of the maid by a bourgeois gentleman in the presence of his blind wife. The light rattan furniture of the set, the accompanying piano tunes, the white garden furniture, as well as the white interior of the restaurant and the antique furniture of the hotel room where Voznesenskaya is staying, all serve as reminders of a rich and luxurious past. The world of the film crew is the world of the past, the world of domestic pleasures and style.

After the interrupted film screening Olga is next seen shooting a new film in the studio. She cannot play without her partner (and lover) Maksakov, who has stayed in Moscow, and there is also no film stock. The director of the film, Kaliagin, played by the actor Alexander Kaliagin, is portrayed with irony. He is rather fat and wants to lose weight; therefore, he tries to swing on a tree or do push-ups, making himself look grotesque in the process. The producer, Yuzhakov, and Kaliagin remember the Russian countryside, identifying central Russia as the space they miss, contrasting the green grass of the Archangel region in October, pregnant with the smell of mushrooms, and the environs of Marfino in November, where they had filmed *War and Peace* in 1913, with the heat and the dryness of Southern Russia. A melancholic tune ('Adieu') accompanies these scenes of the recollection of a happy past. The producer targets the actor Kanin, eccentric and with a high-pitched voice, with a view to casting him instead of Maksakov. Another film crew, more fortunate with film stock, is shooting a scene about a female captive at the beach, as its director, Boyma, is carried through the water.[18]

The Whites enter the set, interrupting the making of the film: they have come to check on people, with Fedotov making some courteous enquiries and apologising about the lack of comfort in the town and his intrusions.

Fedotov feels at ease and at home when he is with the crew, behaving in the same way as they do in his concern with his appearance and small compliments. After all, as a White he defends the bourgeois comforts from the communists in Moscow, who wish to remove them. Fedotov is an ardent admirer of Olga, who has deduced from her observations cameraman Viktor Pototsky's involvement with the Revolutionary cause, and covers for Viktor (played by Rodion Nakhapetov, who was famous for his portrayal of strong-minded characters) by confirming his presence on the set during the day.

The bourgeois world of the crew is a safe haven, protected by the Whites, but a spy is hiding here too (like the spy in the headquarters of *At Home Among Strangers*). Olga's conversations with Viktor take place outside the artificial and cocooned world of the film set, when she goes for a ride in the car with Viktor. First, Olga drives with Viktor to the botanical gardens, where they take a stroll. She reminisces about the past, Moscow and Maksakov, the times when she had a role; now she has no work and feels superfluous. It emerges that Viktor was in the hospital where Olga's husband died, leaving Olga alone with two children. Viktor is explaining the new world order when a storm comes up; Olga plays with her shawl in the wind, not listening to his words. Having been driven around and lulled by the talk about the Revolution drowned by the wind (underlining the insignificance of words when compared to deeds), Olga takes the wheel and steers the car off the road. In terms of political awareness Olga has opened her eyes, and is ready to perceive the world around her.

A train from Moscow arrives with rare film stock and the news of Maksakov siding with Gorky and the Bolsheviks. Olga, disappointed, seizes a copy of the journal *Kino*, but finally leaves it on the train when she realises the irrelevance of what they are doing in the provinces. Olga, like the rest of the film crew, leads a splendid life outside political reality. She can think only of screen reality. The filming can continue, and in black and white we see the seduction of the maid as the countess enters: the film is about the past, about an old, bourgeois lifestyle.

During the second ride in the car with Viktor, Olga wants to leave for Paris as she realises the discrepancy between the screen world and the reality that surrounds her, but she is unable to change her life. Her attempt at a public confession about the shallowness of cinema ends in her triumph as she bathes in the crowd of admirers. Nobody wants to listen to her, but everybody wants to look at her. The happy past, the recognition she longs for, is restored for a moment, accompanied by a melancholic tune. Olga now realises the discrepancy between the illusion of the film world and the reality outside.

Kanin makes an appearance in costume similar to that of Ivan Mosjoukine [Mozzhukhin] in Epstein's *The Lion of the Mongols*, reminding us of the historical time.[19] The shooting is interrupted by a search by the Whites for an illegal film on executions of Bolsheviks by the Whites. Olga removes the reel from Viktor's car under the cover of her daughter's doll's pram. Olga wants to do something real, as she exists only on film. Viktor uses her longing without making any attempt at convincing her of the political aims he is fighting for. During the third ride in the car Viktor invites her to a film screening of the documentary footage about the atrocities of the Whites, and again she is concerned with decorum and dress. The film shows documentary footage of the life of peasants, of the arrest of a newspaper editor and the beating of the worker Trofimenko (the scene that took place at the beginning of the film), and of executions. Responsible for all these acts is Captain Fedotov and the Whites, former tsarist officers. Olga sees the real world in the medium that she understands best: film. Joan Neuberger has identified the car as the space for Olga's political education, and the three trips as the three stages of recognition, apprehension and agency. Indeed, these three stages are not unlike the three frames of the statue of the lion in Eisenstein's *The Battleship Potemkin* with the lion waking, rising, roaring. Neuberger argues that Olga remains almost silent after the screening of the documentary footage, taking action rather than relying on words.[20] In fact, the power of the word is undermined throughout the film: the scriptwriter has a crisis, and the words on the Revolution are less convincing than images.

The love story between Olga and Viktor is rather unconvincing. Viktor is stylised in the same way as the other characters from the film crew, and speaks with the same mannerisms about the reality that surrounds them and that the film crew tries to eclipse. In this sense he, too, is part of their world. It is hard to believe that he loves Olga, as he is seen using her charm to protect his films. The stylisation of character makes them so distanced and unreal that the love story one would expect from a melodrama seems unlikely. Olga may love Viktor, or live in the illusion of loving him, dreaming of a family and happiness, but she can think only in categories of film and admiration for her as a star, and therefore thinks Viktor is jealous of Maksakov. They are in love with the illusions of each other: Viktor sees in Olga the beauty of the past lost in the present, while Olga sees in Viktor a connection to the present without, however, being willing to give up her past. Moreover, when Olga learns that Maksakov has turned to Bolshevism she projects her love for him onto Viktor as the next available man who confesses his Bolshevik belief to her. She projects her love onto Maksakov, then onto Viktor, and once she becomes an agent and carries the film in the hatbox, the object of love dies and she acquires a political identity of her own. Indeed, the confusion of her lovers' faces is demonstrated to the spectator by the poster of Maksakov in the studio, which is a picture of Nakhapetov (the actor playing Viktor).

Olga boards a train, intending to return to Moscow; she is forced to stay when Yuzhakov carries her children off the train. The children have simply the function of asserting Olga's role as a mother; they are needed to make her stay in the Crimea, and she uses their toys to retrieve the film from Viktor's car. She runs away from the screen image of reality, not from reality itself; she runs towards a reality she does not know (starvation and Civil War in Moscow). Kaliagin, as superficial as he may seem in his occupation with his size, is the only person to be truthful to her: 'I do understand you. What we are doing is terrible, so trite and stupid' – filming when there are things a man could do.

Olga meets Viktor in a café and asks him to be patient with her love. They talk at cross purposes as Viktor just wants to leave the film with her. A moment later he is shot in his car on the square. Olga searches for love; Viktor for conspiracy. Viktor seeks in her a conspirator but adores her beauty, not her political views. 'Never mind the truth, Olga Nikolayevna, what matters is beauty,' Viktor says trying to reassure Voznesenskaya. Neuberger argues that Olga does not see, while Viktor sees too much.[21] Indeed, Olga mostly plays a blind woman in the films, while Viktor as the cameraman sees everything through the lens of the camera.

After his death Olga tries to give the container with the film to the Bolshevik Ivan (played by Mikhalkov), whom she has met earlier in a restaurant with Pototsky. Ivan turns her away, afraid to be discovered. The film crew prepares for departure, dismantling the set. Captain Fedotov arrives to search the studio, posing an imminent threat to Olga, who is still hiding Viktor's film. A suicide scene is to be rehearsed, and instead of shooting herself Olga fires a blank shot at Fedotov. At this moment the Revolutionaries enter the set to collect the film from Olga. Lebeshev's camera immediately changes to black and white, enhancing the documentary value of the sequence. They kill Fedotov and his officers, and Ivan takes Olga to a tram and sends her to the city, to safety. However, the tram conductor entrusted with her safety abandons the car, joins a group of Cossacks on horseback, and leaves Olga careening through the fields in the yellow tram. The images of the tram chased by the Cossacks echo the Western-style chase of a train from *At Home Among Strangers*. The song 'Where are you, Dream?',[22] composed by Eduard Artemiev to the poem by Mikhalkov's mother, Natalia Konchalovskaya, rehearses the pining for love and accompanies the final image of the film. Olga's destiny remains uncertain as the train disappears in the mist and the Cossacks close in.

If any doubt remains about Mikhalkov's support for the Bolsheviks, then the last and final proof is the role in which he cast himself: a Bolshevik, wise in his decisions, never risking the life of a woman, gentleman-like in manners, who leads the men into the studio to carry out the liquidation of the Whites and of their cruel Captain Fedotov, a former tsarist officer.

Revolution and love are treated as synonyms: the sexual seduction in the old world is replaced by the political seduction accomplished by Viktor to bring Olga to the side of the Revolution; Olga's suicide in the film of the old world is substituted by the surrender of her life to the ideal of Bolshevism: she saves Viktor's film, and travels herself towards a new life. Revolution is love in a public space, not private. Both love and the Revolution are infectious (Maksakov has caught the 'bug' of the Revolution) and forceful (the wind that convinces Olga of her love for the Revolution).

Mikhalkov makes a subtle comment on the nature of film: the screen reality is false, artificial, trite. It is not worth living for. The documentary image captured by the Revolutionary Viktor Pototsky is worth dying for: he sacrifices his life for the making of the film, and Olga is prepared to do the same. The character of Olga is not explored psychologically, but – assisted by Solovei's stylised performance – it is rendered as a type in a melodrama. Olga fails to see the reality that surrounds her, but she searches for ideals of art and beauty. Art thus distracts her from political reality, and cinema (as an art form) is exposed as a distraction. Likewise, silent film is ridiculed: there is no script, no film stock, the actress has no partner, the plot is conventional and stereotypical, cinema makes the masses cry; in short, the film is no work of art but a commercial venture. Although the crew is parodied, they are consistent in their belief in their own ideal, just like the Revolutionaries, except that cinema's ideal is frivolous when set against the backdrop of political and historical reality. Mikhalkov has a stab at art as an artificial and false medium, and, in Neuberger's words, 'exposes our reluctance to engage with the real world'[23] – a theme that he would develop later.

Mikhalkov makes interesting use of black and white inserts. The silent film shown in a cinema at the beginning is screened in black and white; then the scenes being filmed in the studio are shown in black and white; finally, Viktor's documentary footage is black and white. When the Revolutionaries enter the set, reality is immediately turned into history by the use of black and white: the present is history already. In his use of black and white and colour shots, Mikhalkov comments on the medium of film to support the Revolution. He deploys this device much more consistently here than in his previous film, *At Home Among Strangers*.

The decorum and frivolous lifestyle of the film crew is a thing of the past, associated with the melancholic music ('Adieu'); as nice and beautiful as it may be, it is empty. The Whites are intruders, both in the cinema and on the set; they cheat (the tram conductor) and are cruel (Captain Fedotov). The Bolsheviks are gentlemen-like throughout: they protect, charm, assist. Mikhalkov presents a politically correct view of the Revolution as bringing a peaceful change to an old order, with cruelty and violence committed by the

Whites, while the Reds only shoot when there is a threat. The Revolution is to be hailed, Maksakov is indirectly praised for staying in Moscow and siding with Gorky, while the crew is making a film that nobody will want to see, about a lifestyle long past, on the southern borders of Russia. In the historical reality of 1917–1921 film actors and directors were moving south (Mosjoukine, Protazanov, Ermolieff) and would emigrate to Paris and continue to work there, forming the Albatros studio in the 1920s. Mikhalkov's account is not only concerned with the dream factory, 'the conflict between the sweet dreams of cinematography, and the cruel reality that surrounds it',[24] but also with the myth of the past: 'the film is oriented not towards the reality of the 20s, but towards a myth'.[25] This myth is remembered with an ironic nostalgia; in Boym's terms, a nostalgia that 'emphasises the longing and acknowledges the displacement of the mythical place without trying or rebuild it'.[26]

Whereas *At Home Among Strangers* experiments with the genre conventions of the Western and the adventure film, here Mikhalkov explores the genre of the melodrama. It is noteworthy that all these genres were among the most popular film genres in the Soviet Union.[27] Mikhalkov re-invents the genre by transposing it from the private into the public sphere.

> In *Slave of Love*, narrative, mise-en-scène, and art production combine to depict the morally ambiguous end of bourgeois life and commercial cinema as a mirror for the resurgence of commercial cinema and bourgeois pleasure in late-soviet, post-Stalin society. In both cases, a life of private pleasures and individual emotions came into conflict with public responsibilities and a heroic, collective, and utopian spirit. *Slave of Love* suggests that when either one is valorised at the expense of the other, something critical is lost and both the collective and the individual suffer as a result.[28]

Slave of Love received praise in Soviet film criticism for abstaining from an outright condemnation of the film people's inertia but instead offering a revisionist and nostalgic view of the role of cinema in the years immediately following the Revolution. Elena Stishova has argued that the film is oriented not towards the reality of the 1920s but towards its myth.[29] The clash between film and reality makes the petty bourgeois concern with comfort seem farcical without condemning it. Mikhalkov manages to refrain from an authorial voice on the events of the Civil War and the Revolution. It was awarded a prize for best direction at the International Film Festival in Tehran in 1976.

* * *

In his first films Mikhalkov explored the theme of responsibility for action, condemning irresponsible conduct and praising honest and upright Revolutionaries who risked their lives for the sake of the common goal, for the ideal of communism, for the realisation of a dream. Mikhalkov shows an idealised view of the Civil War based on myth rather than fact. He uses a secondary source as the basis for his artistic work, thus creating a double distortion. Objects of art – film or painting – distract and fail to contribute to the Revolutionary cause in dwelling on aesthetic rather than moral values. Aesthetic pleasures belong to the past, to a civilisation that is not part of the rough life of the Revolutionaries *à la* Pototsky or Shilov. Art is artificial, and as such not real. In Mikhalkov's early films the attitude to art is ambivalent. Mikhalkov's next films mark a return to the past of a different period, nostalgically bringing back another lifestyle.

In his first two feature films Mikhalkov chose themes associated with the history of the Revolution and the Civil War. His decision to portray the Revolutionary past at the time of stagnation served to remind people of the ideals of the Revolution. The collective spirit of *At Home Among Strangers* found expression in the popular form of the adventure. The critique of the intelligentsia's inertia, not supporting the political cause and laying the blame for the failure of the Revolutionary ideals in contemporary society at the feet of the audience, made *Slave of Love* an ambivalent film. After *Slave of Love* a certain degree of dissent with Mikhalkov arose among Russian film critics, who professed the political correctness of the film but failed – maybe deliberately – to read the film's criticism of the bourgeois tendencies of contemporary society. Mikhalkov playfully explored genres and re-invented the Western and adventure, as well as the melodrama. The work on the style of the pre-Revolutionary period led him to explore the past as a lifestyle rather than as a backdrop for political and social themes. This shift in interest would manifest itself in the films of the next period of Mikhalkov's career.

In this early creative period Mikhalkov also contributed to the Kazakh trilogy about the Revolution: *The End of the Ataman* [Konets Atamana, 1970], *Trans-Siberian Express* [Transsibirskii ekspress, 1977] and *The Manchurian Version* [Mandzhurskii variant, 1989]. Andrei Konchalovsky had, together with Eduard Tropinin, written the script for *The End of the Ataman*, directed by the renowned Kazakh film-maker Shaken Aimanov.[30] The film dealt with the special task of the Red officer Chadiarov (played by Asanali Ashimov[31]), who in 1921 has to kill the ataman Dutov, a collaborator with the Whites. Chadiarov discloses during this operation the spy in the Red headquarters in his Kazakh home town. In order to fulfil this task, Chadiarov, who is a Chinese prince, has to get himself arrested as a spy by the Soviet commander; then he escapes, crosses the border and sides with the ataman, who resides in China. Chadiarov fulfils the secret mission successfully, while its full scale and significance transpire only at the end of the film. In its use of cavalry chases, escapes and hide-outs in the steppe, this film is fully within the genre of the 'Eastern'. The second film in the trilogy, *Trans-Siberian Express*, follows secret agent Chadiarov to the Manchurian city of Harbin, where in 1927 he resides under the pseudonym of Fan and poses as manager of a cabaret. The script for this film was written by Mikhalkov, the film shot by Eldor Urazbaev. Fan is blackmailed by a banker to travel to Moscow with a Chinese passport and in the company of his 'wife' Sasha. He soon discovers a plot to kill the Japanese businessman Saito, travelling on the same train to offer economic collaboration to the Soviet regime. A criminal gang – composed of Sasha, Saito's bodyguard and a journalist – intend to blame the murder on Fan, who will appear as a Soviet secret service (OGPU) agent.[32] Thus, the counter-Revolutionaries will prevent economic collaboration with Japan, while the blame will fall on the Soviet Union. As the train travels through Mongolia and Siberia, Fan works out the plot and, continuing to play the foolish and silly cabaret owner, he sows suspicion among the enemy. Once Fan has debilitated the gang and prevented the crime, the Red officers arrive to arrest the criminals. The film adopts the style of a detective story, with clear references to a Soviet version of *The Orient Express*. There are chases on the roof of the train, not unlike the seizure of the train in *At Home Among Strangers*. The happy image of Chadiarov with his wife Sultanat and his son in the steppe, anticipating the happy family portrait of *Burnt by the Sun*, appears, but such happiness is a thing of the past, for short-lived moments only. In reality the Bolsheviks faced a tougher task: one that would ultimately cost Chadiarov his life when, in *The Manchurian Version*, set in 1945, he is in charge of a hotel for Japanese officials in Manchuria under the guise of Isidzima and is killed as he saves the life of a Japanese prince.

The three films represented an attempt to create, in the popular genre of an 'Eastern' action film, the story of a secret agent's life, bringing out his commitment to the communist cause and underlining the unity in Central Asia with the Soviet empire during the 1920s. Mikhalkov's script is a variation of the theme of *At Home Among Strangers*, but with the central character played by a Kazakh actor, thus enhancing the unity between European Russia and its Asian parts and the integration of Central Asia into the Soviet empire. The entire project of the trilogy with Kazakhfilm is significant for Mikhalkov's attitude to the Eurasian theme and the role of Russia between Asia and Europe. In the context of the Soviet cinema of the 1970s Central Asia was attractive for the detective genre and adventure films, and the popular Soviet film *White Sun of the Desert* [Beloe solntse pustyni, 1970], directed by Vladimir Motyl and scripted by Rustam Ibragimbekov, further underpinned the popularity of Central Asia's exotic settings.

3. 'Retro' as Style: 1975–1980

In the late 1970s the stagnation led to a dearth of activity in Soviet cultural life. Many artists and intellectuals had emigrated in the first half of the decade, when the wave of emigration to Israel had climaxed, ripping a large hole in intelligentsia circles. In 1972 the Leningrad poet Joseph Brodsky had been expelled, and in 1974 Solzhenitsyn was deported from the USSR. In 1970 the liberal editor-in-chief of the leading literary journal *Novyi Mir*, Alexander Tvardovsky, had been removed from office. All these acts of repression were now showing their effects on cultural life, while, in terms of cultural politics, the stifling atmosphere continued. In 1974 the open-air exhibition of modern art in the Moscow suburb Beliayevo was torn down by bulldozers (the so-called 'Bulldozer Exhibition'). In 1975, when Andrei Sakharov was awarded the Nobel Prize for Peace, he was not permitted to leave to receive the prize in Stockholm; in 1980 he was exiled to Gorky (now Nizhny Novgorod) and later placed under house arrest. In 1978 the dissident Anatoli Shcharansky was arrested; the writer Vasili Aksenov was exiled in 1981. In 1979 Soviet troops invaded Afghanistan, causing an official boycott of the 1980 Olympic Games in Moscow by the Americans and several other Western states. Many writers could not publish their works, and instead resorted to the so-called *samizdat* (self-publishing typescripts with carbon paper – in the absence of photocopiers). A last attempt at opposition was manifested through the underground publication of the almanac *Metropol*, uniting works that were not accepted for publication in the Soviet Union. The gloom and doom of the late 1970s was offset, however, by activities in the underground, including studio and amateur theatre and 'private' art exhibitions (the so-called *kvartirnye vystavki*). The songs of the bard Vladimir Vysotsky voiced opposition to the system by addressing taboo issues such as alcoholism and drugs. Film-makers attempted to provide relief through blockbusters that distracted with exotic settings and exhilarating plots.

While the 1960s had been governed by clampdown, censorship and bans, the 1970s saw deportations, exile and house arrest. The time for the dissidents' fight within the country had been superseded by the elimination of opposition from the country. Therefore, feelings of despair and inactivity dominated the atmosphere of the late 1970s, while the issue of the individual's conscience and the question of how to come to terms with the suppression of opposition and the departure of dissidents became the focus of attention.

During these years Mikhalkov's brother made the epic feature *Siberiade* [1978], stretching from the years of the Revolution to the present (the 1970s) and set in a Siberian village. In Konchalovsky's film Mikhalkov played Alexei Ustiuzhanin, a role that summarises the figure of Mikhalkov in the late 1970s. Mikhalkov's appearance comes in the last part of the film concerned with the 1960s and 1970s; thus he is cast as a contemporary character. After army service and study, Alexei returns to his native village on a steamer. His appearance clearly marks him as a stranger, an outsider: he sports a suit with a tie and a panama hat, one of his trademarks since the role of Brylov in *At Home Among Strangers*. Yet his appearance is mocked immediately when he falls into the water as he gets off the steamer. In the village he impresses everybody by his charm, from the old women to the workers who have come with him to drill for oil. Yet he fails to recognise the love of his youth, the girl Taya (Liudmila Gurchenko) whom he once taught the tango to the tune of 'Utomlennoe solntse' ('The Weary Sun') – the tune that would reappear as a leitmotif in Mikhalkov's *Burnt by the Sun*. Alexei works on the site drilling for oil with his comrade Tofik. If no oil is found, the government is threatening to build a hydroelectric station on the site and drown the entire village, in a scenario not unlike that of Elem Klimov's *Farewell* [Proshchanie, 1982]. As Alexei is about to leave the village the oil bursts from the drilling rig, causing an initial explosion, in which he is killed because he tries to save a colleague. It is the first time Mikhalkov plays a Soviet 'hero', whose death is even reported to a government meeting in Moscow.

On a personal level, Alexei is endowed with the typical characteristics of Mikhalkov's characters: he is a womaniser, generous and liberal in his attitudes, but also non-committal. As he fails to propose to Taya, she starts a relationship with Tofik. Alexei learns about this, but nevertheless wants to take Taya with him when he leaves. Even when she tells him that she is pregnant and does not know who of the two men is the father of her child, he is still prepared to go through with his proposal of a life together 'in Sochi'. Mikhalkov's character is just, generous and good-hearted. He is the darling of the village, the guy who does everything right, and who is by this attribute distinct from and aloof to the others, without ever being condescending. The same is, incidentally, true for Mikhalkov the film-maker vis-à-vis his characters.

In his own films Mikhalkov turned to the Russian classical heritage. In choosing a play set in the late nineteenth century Mikhalkov also returned to the pre-Revolutionary lifestyle that had featured as the meaningless, but nevertheless beautiful, past in *Slave of Love*, where set and costumes reflected the ornate style of interior design and the fashion of the 1910s. Such a rich decor stands in contrast to the habitat of the Revolutionaries in *At Home Among Strangers* and features in many of Mikhalkov's later films. In *Slave of Love* the lavish style is associated with the film crew, with artists who lack a political viewpoint or commitment. From now on the decor is equally lavish, the setting gorgeous and nature powerful, but characters are stifled, prevented from realising their ideas by this burden. Style becomes a trap that prevents development: costumes are straitjackets, the set a prison. The enclosure in a living space cluttered with objects from the past stops characters from reacting and developing in the present, and enshrines them in their past. Therefore the concept of space is an important consideration in the discussion of the films in this chapter. I argue here that, while Mikhalkov explored the private/public conflict in his first two films, anchoring the public firmly in a private motivation (the Revolution's success is based on brotherhood and love), now he empties Russian space of its values and exposes its abstract and timeless aspects, using it to monumentalise the past as a place of no return. In Boym's terms he moves away from the ironic nostalgia of his early films towards a more and more Utopian nostalgia, a longing to rebuild a home for Russia.[1] Furthermore he transfers the failed ideals of the nineteenth century onto the failure of Soviet society in the 1970s, laying the blame for inertia and stagnation at the feet of those who had failed to help build the bright communist future.

An Unfinished Piece for a Mechanical Piano

Having worked from original scripts for his first two films Mikhalkov turned to literary adaptations, working closely with his set designer, Alexander Adabashian. *An Unfinished Piece for a Mechanical Piano* is an adaptation of a little-known play by Anton Chekhov, written in his youth (rejected for stage performance by the theatre director Maria Ermolova) and commonly known as *Platonov* or *Fatherlessness* [Bezottsovshchina, drafted 1878/79, completed 1881/1883, published 1923], which raises many themes of his later major plays while being not condensed but, rather unwieldy in its dramatic form. Like Chekhov's later plays it raises issues of a passing social order and the advent of a new period in history. Mikhalkov's film version endowed the play with international renown, while he discarded all the sub-plots. More important, though, is the fact that Mikhalkov extracted from the play the themes of Chekhov's later plays, and dwelt on the ironic and grotesque: his Platonov is not killed in an act of revenge, nor does he commit suicide; instead, he is condemned to an absurd existence.[2] Having explored popular genres, clearly echoed in the audience figures of 23 and 11 million respectively for *At Home Among Strangers* and *Slave of Love*, Mikhalkov now turned to adaptations of classical literature, targeting a festival audience and the intelligentsia more than a mass audience while remaining concerned with the failure of the intelligentsia.

Literary adaptations had become popular in the 1970s both in theatre and film, partly because no approval from the censorship body that had interfered so heavily in artistic production in the late 1960s was needed for these works. Literary adaptations represented largely safe ground, although Anatoli Efros tripped over his absurdist reading of Chekhov's *Three Sisters* and *The Seagull* in the late 1970s, emphasising the lack of meaning in the life of Chekhov's heroes; this was deemed incompatible with socialism, and led to Efros being removed from his post as artistic director of the Moscow Theatre of the Lenin Komsomol.

Andrei Konchalovsky's *Uncle Vania* [1971] is one such rendering of a Chekhov play on celluloid. His adaptation hardly goes beyond a theatrical approach. Konchalovsky sets the entire film inside a house; there is another world outside, which is visible through the windows and the open doors. *Uncle Vania* is a well-made melodrama without a trace of Chekhovian absurdity, concentrating instead on the melodramatic and the emotional relationships between characters.

Uncle Vania would be of little interest as an adaptation were it not for the use of documentary inserts. The film begins with a series of documentary photographs of scenes from Russian life in the 1890s. The scenes of the exploitation of the earth shown on the photos forebode in an apocalyptic vision the end of an era, the end of the Romanovs, the end of nature, the end of mankind. Konchalovsky uses photos as a document of the real world – as opposed to the artificial world in the house, thus referring subtly to the absurdity of the situation that the play creates: the frivolity of everyday melodrama is set against a backdrop of the end of an era. Russia's historical reality of the photos is more tangible than the family's emotional reality; the aesthetic realities (the set, nature) have a more serious quality than the trifles and psychological entrapments of the characters. For the family nothing changes, but Russia stands on an abyss.

While Chekhov's play moves from the outside (the veranda) to the inside, Konchalovsky confines the entire action to the inside. Only once does the camera leave the house, following Astrov's carriage across a field that resembles the barren land on the photographs. Konchalovsky refers to a number of representations of space (maps, documents, pictures), while offering a final panning shot of the wintry Russian forests and thus ending on a representational space: Russia is literally frozen, covered under a layer of frost and snow. If Konchalovsky begins with an empty space and makes the meaninglessness of that space clear, Mikhalkov begins with a spatial composition and empties it of its meaning, only to impose his own meaning onto the empty space. His melodrama is set against the dream of a Russia lost.

Mikhalkov's film begins with a scene in the open: Triletsky plays chess with Anna Petrovna Voinitseva (played by the elegant Antonina Shuranova), the widow of a general and landlady of the estate, as he tells her the story of a visit he paid to the Kalitin family, whose daughter he courted. The conversation between family friend Glagoliev and Anna Petrovna's stepson Sergei Voinitsev overlaps onto the scene before the camera shifts to the fields, where Glagoliev is cutting grass with a sickle. The opening establishes immediately the favourite scenes of Mikhalkov: the open field bordering on a river; the old stone mansion with steps leading up to it; the stucco-decorated windows and the ornate stone

4. *An Unfinished Piece for a Mechanical Piano*, Sergei (Yuri Bogatyrev) and Glagoliev (Nikolai Pastukhov)

banister of the balcony. The first scene also takes the interior comforts and decorations of the house into the open space: a table with a white tablecloth and white china, some wicker-basket chairs and a small table for the samovar have been brought out into the garden. The farcical nature of the situation – pretending to be inside but seated in the garden – is underlined by the dialogue, which is disjointed from the image.

The arrival of the Platonovs is first seen by Triletsky (played by Mikhalkov, donning a panama hat), who observes the surroundings through a telescope from the balcony. The use of this instrument reduces the field of vision captured by the camera, which follows his gaze through the telescope – a device used in *Quiet Day*. From the long shot of groups of people we move to a panning shot into the distance before entering the house. Mikhalkov mocks the trite occupations of the people on the estate in a short, carnivalesque scene that sketches the characters. Platonov's wife Sashenka wears a formless hat and a plain dress, which are contrasted with the elegant hat and lacy dress of Anna Petrovna. Sashenka is a simple woman, while Anna Petrovna is concerned with superficial trinkets. Triletsky fires a shot to greet their arrival, playing the fool. Triletsky's father has been dozing all morning after a glass of Madeira: he is an old man who takes no active part in life and has a weak spot for liqueurs.

Against these representatives of the 'old order' Mikhalkov sets counterpoints of the 'new order'. Petrin, the representative of a new class of former workers who have accumulated wealth, is reading newspapers all the time: in the grass, on the steps, later in the house. The servant Yasha vehemently objects to his treatment: he moans of the landlords' carelessness and lack of hygiene as he fishes a chair out of the overgrown pond. His concern with hygiene has been compared to Stolz's obsession with health in *Oblomov*.[3] Yasha appears out of the mist, is told off by the mistress, and argues that he did not need to come at all. He is told to procure a pig, and instead calls Triletsky a pig. He is impatient when reminded about the gypsy orchestra by Anna Petrovna. Last but not least, he helps himself generously to alcohol. The servants decide as the masters fail to run their lives. These short glimpses of another life give an ironic twist to the laid-back life on the estate.

Everybody knows their roles and the game can begin: all these characters are capable of playing a well-rehearsed game in which the roles are already known. Humour prevails in the game among the older order. Triletsky senior greets Anna Petrovna as 'goddess Diana': when kissing her hand he can smell gunpowder. Triletsky junior sports a clown's moustache and fools around, scaring Sergei. Glagoliev returns with Sergei's wife, Sofia Egorovna (Elena Solovei), from a boat trip and invites everybody to his estate. All this is a prelude to the meeting between Sofia and Platonov (Alexander Kaliagin), old lovers who are now both married to other partners. Sofia remembers Platonov, but fails to recognise him. They have not met in seven years, since he was a student; now he is a schoolteacher, although he never graduated. Sofia enquires about his wider aims, pointing at his incomplete education. Platonov counter-attacks Sofia and introduces his wife Sashenka, with whom he has a son. He again resorts to acting, playing the fool and enacting a comedy without people realising this: they are first serious, then they laugh when Platonov leads them out of the game. Mikhalkov structures the film as a series of carnivalesque interludes (attractions) interspersed with more serious and profound dialogues.

Anna Petrovna's suitor Shcherbuk, who arrives with his two daughters and his small, independent-minded nephew Petia (added to the plot by Mikhalkov), is another attraction. Shcherbuk proclaims his belief in natural historical selection, the primacy of aristocracy over the peasants, the impossibility for the peasants to achieve anything. Mikhalkov parodies his noble status by dressing both daughters in green dresses – a colour Chekhov considered tasteless. As an emancipated woman Sofia refuses Shcherbuk's hand kiss, but he unexpectedly grabs her hand as she holds on to the banister. The grotesque nature of the situation is underpinned by gestures, which parody the spoken words. Deeds contradict words, dismantling the word as an empty shell. Mikhalkov captures precisely and accurately the nature of Chekhov's works, turning to laughter on the verge of tragedy: '… all that would be so boring if it weren't so funny…'.[4]

A scene between Platonov and Sofia sets another serious counterpoint to the grotesque. Sofia refuses to remember the past, while Platonov remembers details of their meetings. Sofia reproaches Platonov for not having transformed words into deeds, while she herself continues – with verbosity – her vision of Russia's future. Platonov's memory is selective: he wants to remember Sofia, but not his past with Anna Petrovna, who shamelessly flirts with him in a hammock while teasing him with her story of Glagoliev's proposal. Sofia proclaims her intention to feed the babies of those women who have to work in the fields and make hay; Sergei wants to support her action and give away his old suits. Platonov mocks their benevolence in the image of the peasants making hay in tailcoats. Sofia comes across as a woman with the expectation that men should change the world; neither Platonov nor Sergei is capable of anything more than a gesture, and she has only words to embrace her vision of the future. All that these characters can do is to continue to play their well-rehearsed roles. When words are turned into deeds they become comic and grotesque. Mikhalkov again mocks the empty shell of words and undermines the narrative through images, as in *Slave of Love*.

As the number of cynic and grotesque episodes increases, the situation becomes tenser. In order to release tension Anna Petrovna reveals the mechanical piano, and asks her servant Zakhar to perform a piece by Chopin. Zakhar plays, and then steps back from the piano, leaving it to play on its own. The naïve and simple Sasha is so impressed that she faints. Triletsky administers sherry and discards the medicine offered by Sofia. Platonov is concerned for Sasha, but angry because she embarrasses him with her naïvety. Anna Lawton interprets the mechanical piano as an image of the victory of the mechanical age.[5] It is a gadget, like the bike in *Oblomov*, the machine in *The Barber*, designed to represent progress within the context of a backward setting, and it lacks human features.

After the climax of the mechanical piano and the anti-climax of Sasha fainting, the atmosphere is cleansed; this is signalled by the onset of rain. A series of attractions follows as the playing of games continues inside the house. They dress up as Caucasians with wigs and hats, and dance and sing. Then they play cards, and Anna Petrovna wins a kiss from Platonov; she refuses to let him sell his card to Glagoliev, who wants to kiss her. A long, embarrassing kiss between Platonov and Anna Petrovna is interrupted by Sergei breaking something. To the music of Nemorino's aria from Donizetti's *L'Elisir d'amore* Shcherbuk impersonates the roaring of a deer: nature and art are played out against each other. The carnivalesque interlude brings relaxation, and the game serves to integrate everybody on equal terms, creating the illusion of a democratic society.[6]

The characters move from the open space on the veranda into the conservatory, and into the inner section of the house for a serious scene. Inside there are wooden floors, rattan furniture, a wooden staircase to the top floor, and walls decorated with peasants' instruments. Further inside the house there is a dark dining room, lit with candles and kerosene lamps. The dark inside appears even gloomier as the camera captures rooms from the inside towards the windows, thus creating a strong opposing light that obscures vision. They move from light to darkness in an inversion of the time of the day: they are in the gloomiest room at the height of the sun. The kerosene lamps and the fireworks provide artificial light as they eclipse the light and expose their true faces. This scene, with the yellow-brown shades of the dining room, has been compared to the style of the painter Leonid Pasternak.[7]

The dinner scene brings out the real features of the characters, when masks fall: Triletsky, who is a doctor, has no sense of responsibility and sends the worker Gorokhov away when he comes to ask him to see to a sick woman. Petrin, the son of a worker, openly declares that he paid for the dinner as Anna Petrovna is bankrupt. Shcherbuk, convinced of the superiority of the nobility, leaves the table while Anna Petrovna proposes a toast to Petrin, who has enabled her to keep the estate at the price of her honour. Platonov tells a story, disguising his past with Sofia in fiction. Sofia and Platonov were once in love, when they were students; then she left for the capital (St Petersburg) and did not return for a long time. He waited for her, then gave up his studies as his life had been ruined. Yet he never made any attempt to follow her, either. The use of fiction to disguise the truth parallels the use of a film within a film in *Slave of Love* and anticipates the use of the fairy tale in *Burnt by the Sun* to reveal the truth about Kotov and Mitia, pointing to Mikhalkov's firm belief in myth and legend over and above historical fact.

The fireworks are intended to offer another attraction. In a sequence that is black and white for no obvious motive, Platonov (trying to catch up with his past) runs after Sofia to the lake; he reproaches her for having let herself sink so low and marry the idle Sergei. As the camera pans out, it emerges that Sergei has inadvertently been watching them, bringing a cloak for Sofia. The film returns to colour as the upset and humiliated Sergei wants to leave wife and estate and asks for carriage and horse; he is given only a carriage. Platonov runs into the field, accused by Glagoliev of destroying his happiness with Anna Petrovna. He returns to the house, where Sofia is ready to leave with him, effectively proposing the destruction of both their marriages. As he opens the door and goes inside, he declares that 'it won't work', without

5. *An Unfinished Piece for a Mechanical Piano*, Sashenka (Evgeniya Glushenko) and Platonov (Alexander Kaliagin)

clarifying whether he means the door or living together. Platonov screams out that, at 35, his life is over. He runs to the lake and jumps in, attempting suicide, but at its shallowest spot. Sasha comforts him, wraps him in her shawl and caresses him. Nemorino's aria from *L'Elisir d'amore*, played earlier by the little boy on the gramophone, accompanies the scene. As the camera pans out Sergei is seen sitting in his carriage, asleep, without a horse, while Platonov stands in the shallow water swaddled in a woman's shawl. Platonov is no victim of Sasha's shot, as in the play, but of her excessive love. This finale underlines visually the characters' inability to take meaningful action: all that they are capable of is creating absurd and ridiculous scenes, enacting roles but taking no action. The melodrama is brought about by the discrepancy of emotion and action, not public and private life.

The film's final shot lingers on Shcherbuk's nephew Petia, asleep on the sofa. He featured before in white in the fields, flattening the grass; on a bike as Platonov and Sofia talk inside the house; and mischievously playing tricks when the adults are inside. 'We notice his non-childlike exaltation and easily discern in him the feeling of the contemporary town-dweller, experiencing each year a greater and sweeter torture from the longing for another meeting with nature.'[8] The boy does not seek the company of adults and never takes notice of their remarks about his conduct. He stands aloof from the trite concerns and grotesque behaviour that reign in the adult world. He is at one with nature, reared by nature rather than educated, like Iliusha Oblomov. The child in the vast fields of provincial Russia is an image that links Petia to Oblomov but that also becomes emblematic of Mikhalkov's notion of Russia. The concern with the vast field in the final shot is continued from *At Home Among Strangers* and *Slave of Love*, but in this film a child features in this space for the first time. The child is protected inside the house, caressed by the first rays of the rising sun, while chaos dominates the relationship of the characters who have now moved outside, having 'lost' and abandoned the fight for the estate and instead turned onto their union with nature. Mikhalkov fills the space of Russia, emptied of values, with the figure of a child, representing the future; but that child is blissfully asleep. Mikhalkov thus comments on the grotesque behaviour of adults and, simultaneously, the inactivity and somnambulism of contemporary Russia.

Platonov may have given the English version of the play its title, but he is in no way the central character or a hero. Platonov is cynical and resigned to having, once and for all, lost the ideals he harboured in his youth by succumbing to tradition: marriage, child, job. Some characters still have such ideals, such as Shcherbuk in his views of the aristocracy or Sofia in wanting to help the peasants, although these ideals are mocked as empty words. Others have long given up believing in ideals, but pretend that nothing has changed: Anna Petrovna runs the estate as though she has plenty of money, and Triletsky plays at being a doctor for the sake of appearances, but without caring for the sick. Platonov alone realises that he has wasted his life, without ever regaining the possibility of making his ideals come true. He is a genuinely unhappy man, who exposes the false games of the other characters wherever possible. These other characters speak about the fate of Russia without even being capable of taking their own lives into their hands. They express ideas, empty philosophies, without ever acting accordingly. Their stasis in action is juxtaposed to mental flexibility: their imagination allows them to invent themselves in different games, contributing to their grotesque behaviour. Platonov is alive, while all others wither away. Platonov is aware of acting rather than effecting real change, like Mitia in *Burnt by the Sun*. In this sense Platonov may be worse than other characters, but he is not complacent. He mocks others out of dissatisfaction with himself, which makes his behaviour farcical rather than aggressive. Platonov suffers from a mid-life crisis, like Oblomov: neither have their lives ahead of them any more. Yet Platonov is aware of the lie and the deceit, and miserably fails to live up to the responsibility of changing things, at least as far as his own life is concerned. Mikhalkov uses the stasis of the Russian society of the late nineteenth century to comment on the stagnation of the intellectual life in his own period.

Mikhalkov develops several themes from the early Chekhov play that are pertinent to the writer's mature work, especially the master-servant relation and the theme of the former serf taking over the property, which is developed fully in *The Cherry Orchard* (1904). The ideals of Russia's tradition and national heritage are captured in a lifestyle that is about to disappear, adding a melancholic touch to the portrayal of the Voinitsevs. In terms of narrative Mikhalkov uses a story within the story to explore Platonov's past relationship with Sofia, underlining his interest in memory. The return to the past in the scene by the lake is moved into black and white, while colour remains reserved for the present, as it is in *At Home Among Strangers*. A novel element is the concern with the child as bearer of a new life, taking a rest as the crisis ends in stalemate. While Sergei is immobile, sleeping in a lone carriage without horses and unable to leave Sofia, Platonov is saved by Sasha, the bearer of hope and faith, the personification of the Russian soul.[9]

Mikhalkov raises the issue of man's responsibility for his action (or inaction) without ever being condescending. Instead, as one critic has argued, he proceeds 'from debunking to reflection...about man's moral values, about his responsibility before himself and society'.[10] The characters cannot even change their own lives, though they ponder over the fate of Russia. It is the inability to act together with the dream of change that creates the main incongruity in the film, giving rise to its farcical nature. 'The alarming irony of the film's finale lies in the fact that everything remains as it was, as the landlady says. All revolts, arguments, threats of divorce and attempts of suicide end in nothing.'[11] The critics have addressed the issue of the film's fidelity to Chekhov, noting the farcical tone of the film, but they have failed to infer the significance of the critique of inactivity to contemporary Soviet society. They commented on the fidelity to the original Chekhov, Chekhov's ambivalent love of the old and admiration for the new, on the 'retro' style that refrained from any moral statements or a condemnation of the past. The intelligentsia knew only too well that they were being criticised; the fact that they were not condemned appeased them. *Mechanical Piano* is probably Mikhalkov's most successful film, unanimously praised both internationally and in terms of critical attention. It is a masterpiece of the cinema of the late stagnation period, even if it is not ranked among the most popular films, such as *At Home Among Strangers*.

In aesthetic terms Mikhalkov explores the manners and style of the grand life of the late nineteenth century at a moment when it is crumbling, adding a certain charm to the little joys and delight of a life in the countryside with the mechanical piano, the samovar, the gramophone. He uses static camera shots rather than elaborate camera movements to freeze these impressions of a lost past, especially when compared to the jerky mobile camera of *At Home Among Strangers*, while in this film the camera remains tranquil and stationary. Mikhalkov here begins his appreciation of a particular lifestyle that was lost during the Revolution. By setting the film both in the open air and inside the mansion, Mikhalkov has scope to explore the Russian landscape and have the camera linger on the beautiful features of the countryside. The house stands on a slight elevation, overlooking the countryside, and assumes a superior position. The mansion is brought to life for one day, before life returns to the boring period of winter, when the house will get boarded up, like the summerhouse in Viktor Slavkin's play *Cerceau* (1985) – a play that offers a modern reworking of the Chekhovian themes, where a group of city dwellers go to a dacha and venture into the landlady's past through letters that they find in the attic. They return to the present realising the need to change, but incapable of doing so. The house functions as a temporary outlet for the memories of the past before life reverts to the everyday flow, without any external changes having taken place – even though they would have been possible. 'The material sphere here equals people, as is only possible in film. It does not dissolve their drama but experiences the drama with the people. That is why I say that the main hero of the film is the Voinitsevs' estate.'[12] Through the treatment of the estate in *Mechanical Piano* a space that contains the values of the past is created: Mikhalkov no longer pines for the past as a time, but the past as a location, taking the first step towards a nostalgia that takes as object not the process (time) but the aim (space).

Mechanical Piano established Mikhalkov as a film-maker on the international market. The film participated in the competition of a Western European film festival and took the Grand Prix at the 25th San Sebastian Film Festival in 1977. It was unanimously acclaimed by Soviet and foreign film critics, and praised for its subtle but free treatment of the original material. The casting is in no way remarkable, but it is instead the ensemble of a variety of exotic characters that creates the atmosphere for the film. *Mechanical Piano* was published as a play, and after the completion of *Dark Eyes* in November 1987 Mikhalkov directed a production of the adaptation at the Teatro di Roma (Rome).

Five Evenings

In his next film Mikhalkov attempted to recreate the charm of a post-Revolutionary Soviet lifestyle, that of the immediate post-war years of the 1950s, a period ridden with communal flats and a chronic lack of living space, while also filled with a sense of victory – and loss – after the Great Patriotic War. The film was made between the shooting of the first and second parts of *Oblomov*, in only 25 days. *Five Evenings* is based on a film script by the Leningrad playwright Alexander Moiseyevich Volodin (1919–2001), written in 1957. The film, shot in black and white, was exposed to an intensified development process in order to create a sepia effect. It scrupulously follows the script, with only very minor divergences, the most important one being the change of location: the film is set in Moscow, while the action in the script takes place in Leningrad.

The script needs to be placed into the wider context, notably of its productions as a stage play in the 1950s at two of Russia's most avant-garde theatres: at the Bolshoi Drama Theatre in Leningrad it was performed by Zinaida Sharko and Efim Kopelian,[13] and at Moscow's Sovremennik Theatre by Liliya Tolmacheva and Oleg Efremov. In the latter production Stanislav Liubshin, who was now cast for Ilyin, played the part of Slava.

The film deals with the visit of Alexander Petrovich Ilyin to Moscow, where he stays with his girlfriend, Zoya. He discovers that she lives opposite the house where he rented a room before the war. He lived there with Tamara Vasilievna, whom he loved, and with whom he corresponded throughout the war. However, he was excluded from the institute, where he studied chemistry and never graduated; he was outspoken about one of his teachers, choosing to tell the truth rather than be silent and make a career.

Ilyin visits Tamara, who does not know about his past; he pretends at first that he is head engineer of a chemical factory in order not to disappoint her expectations. Tamara is now foreman in a factory, living for her work alone and giving all her love to her nephew Slava, whom she has raised after the death of her sister during the war. While pursuing her ideals and trying to inspire Slava to work well, she overlooks the human merit in people: she fails to see in the seemingly silly girl Katia, whom Slava brings home one night, a loyal and honest person. Ilyin probes Tamara's love by announcing that he wants to give up his job and asking her to follow him to the north (he works in Vorkuta). She refuses: work and the social contribution rank highest for her, and she is not ready to return to the feelings she experienced in her past. By the time she discovers the truth about Ilyin, during a visit to his former fellow student Timofeyev, Ilyin has left. In the final episode Ilyin returns to Tamara, who is now ready to leave with him. The heroes play roles for each other, and only when they give these up can they see each other for real.

The film is divided into five evenings. On the first, Ilyin is at Zoya's place and pays a visit to Tamara, who invites him to stay in his old room; her nephew Slava returns with Katia. During the second evening Slava and Ilyin become friends and prepare a surprise dinner, which Tamara refuses, unable to enjoy anything in life. As she hears him sing,[14] Tamara is drawn back to Ilyin. On the third evening, the visit of Ilyin and Tamara to Katia's workplace at the telephone station is omitted (the call to Zoya is made from the flat), as is Tamara's visit to Zoya on the final evening. Tamara and Ilyin return home, where he probes her commitment to him as a person rather than to his job. She admires him for his job, and leaves without farewell. On the fourth evening Tamara visits Timofeyev, who unwillingly discloses Ilyin's secret. On the final evening Ilyin bids farewell to Zoya and Katia (the visit to the telegraph is transferred to this part). Katia follows Ilyin to the railway station's restaurant, where he tries (and fails) to remember a song from the past and she gets drunk with him. She returns to Slava's place, drunk but with a copy of the notes he needed for an examination but which a fellow student refused to share. Timofeyev appears with a present from Ilyin (a large looking-glass), and fixes the heater. Ilyin returns to Tamara and love triumphs.

Five Evenings begins with black and white shots of the university, Moscow and its people and streets, fashion shows. The scenes from the life of the 1950s are set to music, which fades out as the record player slowly runs out of power. Darkness fills the screen as Ilyin fixes the light at Zoya's flat. They look at a fashion journal, before Zoya lays the table and finds her cake burnt. Ilyin notices the house on the other side of the road and leaves, setting the alarm clock, as promised, to be back in ten minutes. When he arrives in the communal flat, Tamara already has curlers in her hair and is wearing a dressing gown. When she eventually opens the door, he enters and behaves like the landlord. The camera lingers on their faces, without following the voice of the speaker. The static camera enhances the tranquillity that reigns in this scene, despite the tense emotions that arise in the characters. The movement takes place within the frame, and does not come from the camera. This requires a particular skill from the actors, found in Mikhalkov's choice of two actors familiar with the psychological realism required for such a drama, Liudmila Gurchenko and Stanislav Liubshin.[15] In its static setting in the communal flat the film lapses into a theatrical mode, echoing the 1950s style of filmed theatre productions that were designed to raise the number of films released, which had dropped to an all-time low after the war.[16]

For Tamara, life consists in work. As in Menshov's Oscar-winning *Moscow Does Not Believe in Tears* [Moskva slezam ne verit, 1980] two years later, the achievement at the workplace is a necessary prerequisite for personal happiness. However, things are more complex in this film. Tamara has very high ideals, and makes high demands on herself and everybody around. She has sacrificed her life for the education of her nephew, so she expects everybody to do the same. Thus, Tamara accuses Katia of distracting Slava from his work; yet her anger is almost calmly enacted rather than ill-tempered. Similarly, her rage at the dinner table, which Ilyin laid for her, reveals more about her self-discipline than her evil nature. She regrets her words later, but never apologises; her regret is merely alluded to when she hears the song from Ilyin's room and the camera closes up on the sad expression on her face. Ilyin is in solidarity with Slava: they cut a deal on making Tamara happy. Ilyin shadow-boxes with Slava, and Slava becomes his friend rather than an adopted child in need of education.

The poverty of the communal flat stands in sharp contrast to Timofeyev's flat, which has just been refurbished and fitted with wooden floorboards, preventing Tamara from coming into the flat where Ilyin is, in fact, hiding. Timofeyev has made a career; he is well off. As he later confesses, he too was silent when he should have shown a strong character, like Ilyin. The exposure of abuse of power was in line with the 1950s ethos, the period in which the play was written and set. Mikhalkov here comments on the period of the 1950s as a time when political expediency was rewarded, while honesty was punished. He implies that, in the 1970s, this had changed.

Tamara neglects herself: Zoya is concerned with appearance, looking at fashion journals, and immediately changing her shoes when Ilyin visits her at work. Katia wears a white cap (a so-called *meningitka*, a cap covering the meninge – the back – of the head) and matching little scarf when she visits on the second day. Tamara only realises that she was wearing a gown and had curlers in her hair during the first evening once Ilyin has gone to bed, when she is angry with herself. On the last evening she dresses up in expectation of

Ilyin's return, and Slava remarks on the unsuitability of the white blouse if she wants to do the dishes.

Ilyin is a performer: he plays the guitar, directs the laying of the table for the surprise dinner, performs some dance steps as a farewell to Katia in the telegraph office before kissing the handle of his umbrella. He is happy with his life, even if he has not made a career and gained the material benefits that Timofeyev has. Indeed, Timofeyev's flat is empty, sterile and impersonal, a makeshift space rather than a home. When Ilyin confesses to liking his job, in which he brings goods to people in the region, where he is needed, he has tears in his eyes. He is lying as much as Tamara, who has suppressed her love and femininity but claims to lead a full life: 'The film's sphere is personification, acting, carnival. The world of Mikhalkov's films is always artistic, based on game.'[17] Typically, Mikhalkov resorts to the stylisation of emotions in a game where the rules are known. Both Tamara and Ilyin know what to expect of each other: Ilyin is aware of the need to impress Tamara with his social achievements, and Tamara knows only too well about her unfulfilled personal life. Both delude each other and themselves in these areas. The melodrama draws a division between the public (Tamara) and private (Ilyin) spheres, which are reunited in the finale.

6. *Five Evenings*, Tamara (Liudmila Gurchenko)

The last sequence pans over photos on the walls, small objects on the table, the television and Tamara's face as Ilyin rests his head in her lap. She mutters some words about another life in the future, seeing all the things she has only heard about. The film here raises the trauma of the war; Tamara and Ilyin both remember their farewell before the war, which separated their lives. Tamara still fears the war: 'If only there is no war,' are her final words. The world of their hopes has been destroyed by the war, and is irretrievably lost. It must be built anew as it cannot be restored. Here Mikhalkov offers an honest nostalgia, where the characters are fully aware that they are living in a present that is different from the past, where they long for a personal happiness built on the experiences of the past while acknowledging the present.[18]

In Chukhrai's *Ballad of a Soldier* the soldier Skvortsov is a hero, but he is an ordinary human being when it comes to his girlfriend and his mother. In Shepitko's *Wings* Nadezhda Petrukhina is unable to live a normal life after the heroic feats of the war as a fighter pilot. Mikhalkov taps into this tradition of the Thaw and post-Thaw films about the war, which reviewed the concept of heroism. The film also brings out the impossibility of heroism outside the war: the characters in the film are ordinary people, with the capacity for everyday heroism but not for grand-scale national heroic feats. Thus, the pursuit of truth is worth more than a career. Characters are 'decent' (*poriadochnye*) – no more and no less.[19]

Mikhalkov makes interesting use of the acoustic devices in this film: there is hardly any non-diegetic music. Mostly the television is switched on for the neighbours, who always come to watch a programme at moments when Tamara and Ilyin are emotionally ready to explain their feelings for each other. The neighbours leave when they notice they might infringe her privacy. First they come to hear about the achievements of the Soviet sports teams announced by the presenter Nina Kondratova, and the participation of Van Cliburn in the 1958 Tchaikovsky Piano Competition; then they want to see *Swan Lake*. Timofeyev too is watching the musical comedy 'Spring in Moscow' ('Vesna v Moskve') on television when Tamara arrives. The television set is a KVN-49, a Soviet-manufactured television with a small screen, which could be enlarged with the help of a lens (such as the one Timofeyev delivers to Tamara).

In the communal kitchen the radio is playing during the scene between Katia and Slava, announcing the achievements of the Soviet Union. The reports on both media underline the Soviet obsession with achievement: doing best and coming first. The heroism expected for media coverage has, however, no bearing on the life of ordinary people: it provides a mere background. In the subtlest possible way Mikhalkov provides a critique of the Soviet obsession with social achievement, which can, as we see in this instance, destroy the possibility of personal happiness. The technique he uses is not unlike the device used in Yuri Liubimov's production of Trifonov's *The Exchange* at the Taganka Theatre, where the idealised Soviet world occupies the space at the back of the stage (a performance by skaters) while ordinary people only have the small and cluttered front stage for their lives. Moreover, Tamara plays a tango on the gramophone – a hint at the 'forbidden fruit' of the 1930s, when the tango was deemed harmful and decadent. Ilyin plays guitar and sings, using the most traditional and individual musical expression.

The film's events unfold largely in the communal apartment, reconstructed with all the detail possible: flowery wallpaper patched up by newspapers; a telephone with a long cable in the hall; the divided kitchen space with each family having its own table; crammed rooms and screens to separate public and private space; old furniture and makeshift decor. Mikhalkov extends the 'retro' style (usually referring to the pre-Revolutionary period) to the post-war Soviet period and finds elements of that lifestyle attractive and worth remembering. As Stishova argues, Mikhalkov achieves in this film a careful reconstruction of the past, bringing it closer and turning it at such an angle that we feel its loss.[20] Similarly, Slavkin would remember underground music in *A Young Man's Grown-Up Daughter* [Vzroslaia doch' molodogo cheloveka, 1977], a play that dealt with the habits, the antics and the fashion of the generation of the Teddy boys (*stiliagi*). From the point of view of marketing, the film was successful in other Eastern-bloc countries, while it was deemed unsuitable for export to the West because of its glorification of communal life. Therefore no dubbed or subtitled versions of this film are available, and its international promotion began and ended in the Festival of New Cinema in Hyères (France) of 1979. It received little critical attention at home or abroad.

A Few Days from the Life of I.I. Oblomov

After his success with *Mechanical Piano* Mikhalkov turned to another literary adaptation of a classic work of Russian literature, the novel *Oblomov* by Ivan Goncharov (1812–1891), written in 1859. Goncharov explored in his work the lifestyle of Ilia Ilyich Oblomov, a man of middle age who is incapable of any action. He spends his time on a couch in his St Petersburg flat and lives off the income from his run-down estate, Oblomovka. The novel appeared at a time when literary critics and political thinkers alike were trying to find in fictional characters an argument for or against political change. The radical thinkers, led by Dobroliubov,[21] saw epitomised in *Oblomov* the 'superfluous man', who – as a result of the prevailing feudal system – had degenerated into a vegetable state. Their view was countered by the conservative critics, who stressed Oblomov's poetic features and insisted that his antithesis, Andrei Stolz, was a cold and heartless marionette of progress. The debate around the novel further divided Russian thinkers into two camps, the Westernisers (Stolz) and the Slavophiles (Oblomov), thus creating a fissure between the two characters that precluded any interpretation of the pair as two sides of one coin.

Yet it would seem that this ambivalence, and the duality between Oblomov and Stolz, particularly attracted Mikhalkov to the novel. In *At Home Among Strangers* Mikhalkov had dealt with the conflict between the Revolutionaries and the counter-Revolutionaries, while private considerations nurtured the political success; in *Slave of Love* he had explored political activity anchored in private relations, while remaining ambivalent about the lifestyle of the Reds and the Whites; in *Mechanical Piano* the ambivalence lay in the loss of the past, on the one hand, and in the inactivity of characters vis-à-vis the future, on the other – which is an inherent feature in Chekhov's works. *Oblomov* is also full of ambiguity, and Mikhalkov is not required to take a position, exactly as in the work on Chekhov. However, Goncharov provokes his readers with a painstaking and fastidious description of Oblomov's inactivity, frustrating expectations of action and thereby challenging the reader. Goncharov is a pedantic observer of detail, poking fun at the readers' assessment of Oblomov by wasting hundreds of pages on moving his foot, or mocking Oblomov's slowness and boredom. Mikhalkov selects a few days, thus condensing Oblomov's lethargy into a few hours and, moreover, focusing on a period of relative activity in Oblomov's life, when his boredom is shaken up by the presence of Stolz and Olga respectively. Thus the focus on Oblomov's more active period rather than the farcically lethargic Oblomov casts a more sympathetic light on the figure, assisted further by the casting. In his cinematic interpretation of the novel Mikhalkov clearly comes down on the side of the conservative views: his Ilia Ilyich Oblomov, played by the cheerful and much-loved Oleg Tabakov[22] (one of the founding members of the Sovremennik Theatre and later actor and director at the Moscow Arts Theatre), is a lovable character, never mind his apathy. Yet Mikhalkov's Stolz, played by the good-natured Yuri Bogatyrev, who had played Egor Shilov in *At Home Among Strangers* and Sergei Voinitsev in *Mechanical Piano*, also displays the positive features of a caring and concerned friend.

It is this interpretation that led the critical debate about the film; it was less dominated by an analysis of the film than by a discussion of the position Mikhalkov adopted vis-à-vis the Soviet criticism of the novel. Mikhalkov leads the spectator into the film by showing Oblomov as perceived by the radical, and later Soviet, critics: as an idle product of a society in need of change, a man whose life is run by the equally lethargic and indecisive servant Zakhar. Yet, with the arrival of Stolz, Mikhalkov departs in his portrayal from the orthodox Soviet reading of Oblomov, largely by means of the selection of 'several days' of activity and by the casting. Mikhalkov destroys the myth of Oblomov created by Soviet criticism, together with their glorification of Stolz.

There is very little action in the novel. Mikhalkov selects a few events in Oblomov's life to sketch it: Oblomov at home with his manservant Zakhar, beautifully and comically interpreted by the great actor Andrei Popov;[23] the visit of Alexeyev; the arrival of Stolz and a visit to Olga Ilyinskaya; Oblomov's summer sojourn in a dacha near the Ilyinskys' summer estate, including the baron's proposal to Olga, Olga's confession to him and Stolz's return from Europe; and a final episode, cutting directly to the time after Oblomov's marriage to Pshenitsina and his death, showing the stifled family life of Stolz and Olga, who have adopted Oblomov's son. The details of Oblomov's marriage to Pshenitsina have been completely omitted, as have numerous visits by his Petersburg friends and petitioners.

Mikhalkov's Oblomov is loved both by Olga and Stolz, as well as his manservant Zakhar. Oblomov is funny in his social ineptitude and charming in his naïve and infantile reactions, withdrawing into a corner to sulk when laughed at in Olga's house, or cheating himself when having a secret meal in his own kitchen at night while dieting. This infantile feature is not developed

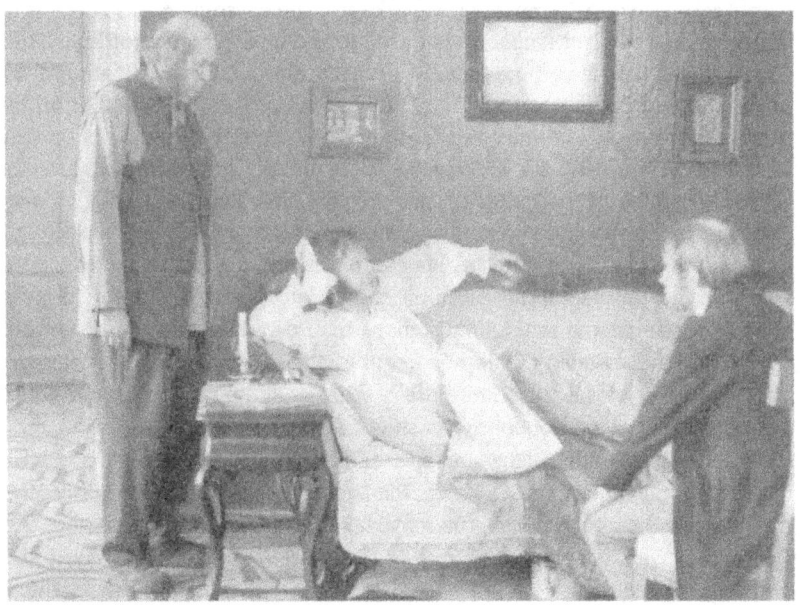

7. *A Few Days from the Life of I.I. Oblomov*, Zakhar (Andrei Popov), Oblomov (Oleg Tabakov) and Alexeyev (Avangard Leontiev)

in the novel. Oblomov takes everything that is said very seriously, for example, when he manually destroys the lilac bush that obscures the view over the valley.

In a series of flashbacks Mikhalkov brings back the childhood of both protagonists to explain their characters, dwelling on the responsibility of parents and society for the education of their children. Stolz had a German father who was harsh and demanding, sending the son away to be educated in St Petersburg. His farewell is cold, while the village community embraces and cherishes the master's son. Stolz never experienced parental warmth, and was instead left to fend for himself in society. Oblomov's childlike behaviour tallies with his protection of his own childhood in his flashbacks and his unwillingness to grow up, which is manifest in his weepy character: Oblomov is, for example, so moved by Stolz's words in the sauna that he almost cries with self-pity.

Mikhalkov's Stolz is more despotic than Goncharov's. The Stolz of the film will help Oblomov only if he surrenders to his plans and threatens Oblomov with the withdrawal of his friendship and company otherwise. Yet he waives his rigidity when Oblomov does not comply with his requests (the meal, the snow bath and the bicycle). Indeed, much of the film's criticism was levelled at the positive portrayal of Oblomov (a figure incompatible with Socialist Realism) and the denigration of Stolz's constructive approach to life, which could seriously have hampered the film's fate with censorship. Stolz manages his own life, and places much importance on physical fitness according to the motto 'mens sana in corpore sano'.[24] He eats fresh vegetables and fruit instead of a stodgy diet of bread and fats, and cares for his blood circulation by rolling in the snow after the sauna. Stolz is busy in everyday life, not only in terms of his business. His ideals for a better life are simple and achievable. Oblomov's lethargy is apparently caused by his early childhood, when he was pampered by his loving mother and cherished by the servants. Yet his activity has no aim or meaning; thus his life culminates in boredom in the end.

Both Stolz and Oblomov have the capacity to forgive. Oblomov forgives Zakhar for doing and saying things that a manservant is not supposed to do. Similarly, when catching Oblomov feasting in the kitchen at night during his diet, Stolz laughs and joins him. Both in terms of actions and character, Stolz and Oblomov are neither entirely positive or negative characters. Rather, they complement each other. They are representative of a certain type of character and of political views in the 1860s: the Westerniser and the Slavophile, the radical and the conservative, the material and the metaphysical figure. As Neya Zorkaya has commented, in the sauna scene Oblomov addresses the philosophical question of 'why live?' while he classifies Stolz with those people who explore the materialistic issue of 'how to live'.[25]

Oblomov is capable of action, but needs to be supported in his activity constantly: it suffices for Olga to miss a rendezvous, or for Stolz to travel abroad, and Oblomov lapses back into lethargy. Oblomov only twice refuses to join Stolz: when he should jump into the snow after the sauna, and when asked to ride the bike; both involve physical exercise. Without support he surrenders to inactivity and ultimately dies. However, there is also society that surrounds Oblomov, and here Mikhalkov feeds in some views held by the more radical polemicists of the time. There is nothing for Oblomov to do in the society of Nicholas I's Russia: his estate almost runs itself, and he is bored by the small talk in St Petersburg society, both at the party at Ilyinskaya's house and when paying a visit to an official with Stolz. Tabakov's Oblomov might be inclined to act, to take responsibility, but there is nothing that demands his attention, social soirées are façades, and neither politically nor socially is any action – not to mention change – desired. His inactivity and lethargy is by choice and not genetically conditioned:

> Oblomov does not take part in Stolz's rush of life because he is lazy, but because he has an organically different link to the surrounding world [...] Oblomov's rejection of any activity whatsoever in the film is reflected and programmatic, a characteristic of a conscious non-desire to adopt the imposed rules of the game.[26]

In the sauna scene Oblomov explains that he is no teacher, that he has no intention of promulgating any thoughts or ideas or multiplying his property,

8. *A Few Days from the Life of I.I. Oblomov*, Oblomov (Oleg Tabakov) and Stolz (Yuri Bogatyrev)

that he dislikes society and its superficial activities. Stolz reproaches him that he is not needed in society and has himself to blame for the absence of such a role. Again, Mikhalkov is concerned with rules of the game and the playing of roles in society. His Oblomov is an outsider by choice. Mikhalkov comments on Soviet society in the 1970s and declares that action is pointless, after his fruitless appeals for action and his criticism of lethargy in earlier films.

Oblomov is capable of socialising with a small group of people, but not with society at large, which he finds repulsive. In fact, on his first visit to Ilyinskaya's house he leaves the room, having been sidelined and mocked by the guests. It is only when Olga talks to him in person and alone that he is willing to return. In this sense, Oblomov suffers from a form of autism: he is capable of relating to individuals, but not interacting with groups. Moreover, St Petersburg is cold, gloomy and depressing, and there is no attraction in the city that makes it desirable for Oblomov to leave the warmth of his flat. The image of a city that drives people to depression, so common in nineteenth-century Russian literature, is hinted at, especially since Mikhalkov's Oblomov is a more cheerful person altogether once he lives in the countryside. In this aspect Mikhalkov plugs into the tradition of interpreting St Petersburg as a depressing and gloomy city, leading to madness and crime.

Mikhalkov makes a significant addition to *Oblomov*: Stolz returns from Europe with a new invention, the bicycle, which may be seen as a sign of progress, although it features only as a harmless toy and an object for entertainment in the boring countryside. An attraction is introduced to ease tension, as with the mechanical piano. However, whether Mikhalkov is critical of Russia's backwardness or of Western progress is debatable. In *Dark Eyes* Romano visits Russia, yet his role as a Westerner who brings progress to a backward country is not developed: his sale of unbreakable glass is only a pretext, and he has no intention of building a factory. The perennial concern with nature in Chekhov's work is only a secondary theme for Romano, and for the film-maker.

The final episode of the film gives reason to doubt that Stolz's life is happier: he seems to be stifled in his family life without much enjoying the children he has with Olga. The idealism and enthusiasm of his youth has gone, giving way to the sedate existence of a family man. And without Oblomov to balance his materialism and striving for progress he leads only half a life. Neither Stolz nor Oblomov are models in Mikhalkov's reading of the novel, even if his sympathy lies with Oblomov.

Lebeshev's camera lingers on the Russian landscape of Kostroma, both for the Oblomovka sequences in the flashbacks and the shots of the woods and fields surrounding the summerhouse. Oblomov's destruction of the lilac bush to offer a wider view of the fields takes a prominent place in the film, revealing Oblomov's thoughtless conduct vis-à-vis nature to achieve a perfect, picturesque view of a beauty spot. The artistic impression is more important to Olga than the chaos that nature offers. This vision, though, is replicated by the film-maker, who also seeks to elevate nature above pure representation and to establish its monumentality.

At the end of the film the camera pans over the vast space of a Russian valley as a boy runs in a field towards a river, a scene accompanied by Rachmaninov's *Vespers*. The green fields and woods with a river quietly flowing through a valley represent Mikhalkov's favourite image and his ultimate symbol for Mother Russia. It echoes a view of his own childhood over the river near his home on Nikolai's Hill (Nikolina Gora).

> The space is dynamic in this frame. As if with elasticity he jumps and moves away from our gaze, and with each jump the frame acquires more scale. The boy does not reach his mother; the distance that opens in its depth moves the caressing embraces of loving hands beyond reach. But the distance itself is happy and bright like a smile.[27]

The image of a child in the field represents nostalgia for a Russia of the past. The sequences suggest Russia's expanse, its vastness, but also – through the association with a child – its immaturity and, in the context of the narrative, the inability of characters to be at one with the present: they idealise a Russia of their childhood, a cocooned existence, the dream of a return to a sheltered past. In Boym's terms, the past is reconstructed in the final shots from a spatial and temporal distance that is not acknowledged, repeating the past in the here and now. Mikhalkov is here deploying a restorative view of the past, recreating it as a Utopia, without the ironic distance and the recognition of the displacement that informs his earlier films.[28]

When Russia is viewed from a distance, or from abroad, the degree of idealisation is enhanced. Oblomovka is a childhood memory as well as an estate at a distance. In Tarkovsky's *Nostalgia* the Gorchakovs' wooden house is not only in the past but also in the distance, and it is simultaneously in the present and in Italy, surrounded by ruins. Tarkovsky transposes his image into the here and now, while Mikhalkov deludes himself and the spectator to believe in a perfect Russia of the past, the lost paradise of the nineteenth century.[29] It is with *Oblomov* that the retreat into the nineteenth century as a Utopian nostalgia begins. Mikhalkov 'totalizes' (Boym) the vision of the home, the country and Russia's heritage.

If Konchalovsky offers a non-idealised view of Russia, choosing pictures of the past (*Uncle Vania*) to point at the devastation of Russia's countryside and admitting that Mother Russia is only a visual ideal that does not hold up to scrutiny by a Western eye (*Nest of Gentlefolk*), then for Mikhalkov the image of Mother Russia (the child in the field with a river flowing quietly through a valley) is indestructible because it belongs to the past while failing to acknowledge the present. Mikhalkov here anticipates his Russian nationalism, explicitly rendered in his later films, and his wish to return to the late nineteenth century without realising that his version of the past is distorted and not suitable for the present. He constructs his own Utopian homeland as he builds his very own family genealogy. Mikhalkov freezes these images of Russian nature: the view of the valley is frozen as Andriusha continues to shout for his mother. It is the act of freezing the frame that instils a sensation of timelessness, of monumentality in the space, which possesses a value as harbouring pastoral values and traditions of the past; yet the link to the past has been severed. The space is disconnected from reality, but neither is it imaginary; instead, Mikhalkov substitutes real for virtual and vice versa, creating an empty, disconnected space that is filled only by the sound of the *Vespers*.

Such images of the landscape also appear at the beginning of the film, when etchings of St Petersburg monuments are superimposed onto the views of the landscape. This device suggests that symbols have been imprinted onto nature, that change in Nicholas I's Russia is an illusion, a vision only, scratching the surface of a façade. Urban space is a mere reproduction, as opposed to the three-dimensional quality of rural space. The etchings gradually subside to the watercolours of Gorokhov Street, of Oblomov's apartment, and then come to life with the characters in a picture animation. Yet this device is not solely limited to the beginning of the film. Stolz's flashback to his childhood also begins with a drawing of a boy by a window as Stolz sits by the window of the *bania* (sauna) and looks out onto a snow-covered plane. The camera moves to a series of paintings showing a boy at a desk, and then with his mother, before the narrative of Stolz's childhood has reached the moment when he leaves the estate, and the flashback switches to filmic representation.

At the same time it is a comment on art, which freezes time: the etchings and watercolours are a poor sketch of the city's real beauty. Art is unable to capture the view of the landscape, and the destruction of the lilac bush to create an artistic view is childish and negative. Mikhalkov's view of art reaches the climax of ambivalence in *Oblomov*. Western art (painting, etchings, music) is negative and artificial. The 'Casta diva' aria from Bellini's *Norma* that Olga (Solovei) performs is but an artificial entertainment, from an opera much loved in Goncharov's St Petersburg, but not Russian. Rachmaninov's *Vespers* ('Now let Thy servant part, oh Lord'), associated with the innocent and unspoilt boy, is Russian and not mangled by civilisation and society. Mikhalkov treats Western art as an artificial product while Russian art is genuine, inverting the view of the Marquis de Custine that informs Sokurov's *Russian Ark* [Russkii kovcheg, 2002], who considers Russian art as a mere imitation of Western culture. Ilya, too, is not crippled by social conventions. He has not been educated, but he has been loved by his mother: 'Ilyusha is not educated, but he grows together with the plants'.[30] The painted view and the sung love story replace reality, and Oblomov temporarily trusts these empty shells more than his recurrent recollection of his childhood. Oblomov is thus a victim of his own aesthetic design, alienated from society and nature as the city is alienated from reality in the watercolours.[31]

Stolz and Olga draw Oblomov into an aesthetic vision of the world that fails them in the end. Oblomov's dream is set against their illusion of reality. Neither world is ideal, and Mikhalkov seems to point at the desirable, but impossible, unity of the two worlds. The film begins with a narration of the storyline as watercolours of famous St Petersburg monuments, with their European architecture, intercept the titles: Annenkov Bridge, the Admirality, St Petersburg's wrought-iron gates and fences, St Isaac's Cathedral and the rostral columns. The images of the city give way to a drawing of Gorokhov Street, and a painting of the flat's interior that then transforms into filmic reality. Film is created through the narrative, on the one hand, and artistic images, on the other. From this view the film creates 'reality'. Life, then, is an animated painting, while life attempts to turn reality into art (artificial). Life is endowed with the static quality of a painting, and thus it cannot develop. Mikhalkov thus juxtaposes the inauthentic aesthetic image to the aestheticisation of life:

> This complex of gestures amounts to a reversal of the temporal flow, the result of which is the stasis of a picture that passes from frame to frame in violation, in a sense, of the medium. It is a forced overturning of the opening sequence and of the process by which the novel was adapted. It is thus simultaneously a return by one step in the process of artificially estheticising life and an implicit recognition of the rigidity and 'inauthenticity' of the esthetic image itself.[32]

Indeed, numerous textual and visual references lead to another Russian classic: Anton Chekhov. The issue of the purpose in life that lies in the purchase of a small estate with a gooseberry shrub stems from the short story 'The Gooseberry Bush'; the obsession with the inappropriateness of a bicycle can be found in the story 'The Man in a Briefcase'; while the seclusion from reality and the unwillingness to participate in it can be detected in the story 'The Wife'.

In returning to the past, Mikhalkov dwells in each of these films on the stifling effect that objects and material possessions have on man when style becomes a burden. The mansion of *Mechanical Piano* leads to a life wasted in meaningless pastimes; the wealth of Oblomov leads to his descent into inactivity; and the objects of the past, photos and furniture, that furnish Tamara's room – even if it is in a communal flat – make it impossible for her to leave. Only when Tamara in *Five Evenings* is willing to leave her rooms in the communal flat does she begin to develop and lead her own life by following Ilyin. Oblomov, too, is comfortable on his divan in his apartment, and rarely and reluctantly has the need or the urge to leave the house, as this would require physical movement and the development of independent action. However, the situation could be turned around: the characters on Anna Petrovna's estate have nothing to do but engage in frivolous and trite activities; nor does Oblomov. Tamara has nothing to hold onto but a few trinkets of a past happiness captured in the photos. Mikhalkov does not condemn decoration, but he goes beyond the surface and explores the meaninglessness of life where the individual has no task, no function, no responsibility. In *Five Evenings*, however, it becomes clear that even function and responsibility (which both Tamara and Ilyin have) do not bring fulfilment.

Permanence lies in the motherland – represented in the images of nature, in the image of the sacrificing and forgiving woman hugging her husband, in the sequence of a child running in the field or sleeping on a sofa. In these films Mikhalkov offers through a series of visual symbols his view of Russia as a place that never changes. Mikhalkov idealises a Russia of the past, and dissolves time in nature images. In Boym's words the shift from *algia* (longing) to *nostos* (home) has been accomplished at this stage in Mikhalkov's work.[33]

For Mikhalkov the image of open landscape encapsulates Mother Russia. In Andrei Tarkovsky's films, too, Russia is rendered through the poetic image of a landscape with a country house (*Mirror*), or a meadow with a hut by a little pond where past and present merge (*Nostalgia*), but Tarkovsky always marks the images as an invention, a place of the imagination. For Konchalovsky this image is always in real time (the past), and as such acknowledged by the characters in their discourse (document or flashback), thus offering an authentic relation of time and space. For Mikhalkov the image of the Russian fields is both in the past and the present. He dissolves and blurs time and space, creating the illusion of a continuous past and, by implication, of Russia's permanence. Mikhalkov halts the continuum of cinematic time. If from the point of view of narrative Mikhalkov's position is ambivalent, then visually it is clearly Russophile.

4. Modern Times: 1980–1985

In the first half of the 1980s a sense of stagnation still characterised the atmosphere in Soviet culture, while politically the period witnessed a rapid succession of Soviet leaders after the death of Leonid Brezhnev in 1982, leading to an expectation of change. Yuri Andropov, former head of the KGB, was in office for a little more than a year (1982–1984), Konstantin Chernenko for less than a year (1984–1985). Neither Andropov's nor Chernenko's reign, therefore, bears clear and definite characteristics in terms of their politics, but suffice it to say here that Andropov appears to have intended a relaxation in cultural politics while Chernenko was more of a hard liner. An example may serve as evidence of this: Yuri Liubimov, working in the United Kingdom in 1983, gave an interview to *The Times*, denouncing petty cultural officials in the hope of providing Andropov with a reason for replacing these officials with more liberal figures. The purpose was missed largely because on the day of the publication the Soviet Union shot down a South Korean airliner (5 September 1983) and all attention was diverted to more urgent and global political issues than dealing with petty cultural officials. Chernenko, on the other hand, excluded Liubimov from the Communist Party and stripped him of his passport within a week in office. Clearly, it was not until the accession of Mikhail Gorbachev in 1985 that any real change could be noticed in the cultural sector. The rise in Poland of the Solidarity movement under Lech Wałęsa in the early 1980s and the subsequent introduction of martial law contributed to the atmosphere of oppression of another cry for liberalisation.

Nevertheless, underground activities were flourishing in these years. There was a revival of jazz groups, such as the Ganelin trio and Sergei Kurekhin's 'Popmekhanika'; numerous popular comedies and melodramas were released, while auteur cinema underwent another period of 'shelving' of works by such film-makers as Alexei German, Tengiz Abuladze and Elem Klimov. Films, of course, had no underground outlet because the medium required technological back-up. In the early 1980s the film industry also witnessed the emigration of Andrei Konchalovsky and Andrei Tarkovsky, while the literary world saw the departure of Vasili Aksenov to the United States. It would seem that cultural activities were either doomed to the underground or else channelled into mass popular culture, especially bearing in mind the renewed popularity of cinema in the early 1980s, triggered partly by the immense success of Menshov's *Moscow Does Not Believe in Tears* both nationally and internationally, with 85 million viewers at home and an Oscar award.

Mikhalkov's activities as scriptwriter and actor in these years also fed into the popular vein. His script for *My Favourite Clown* [Moi liubimyi kloun, 1986], based on a story by Vasili Livanov, was co-written with Alexander Adabashian and filmed by Yuri Kushnerev. It starred the young and relatively unknown Oleg Menshikov[1] in the main part of Sinitsyn. The film, a melodrama with a happy ending, was popular at its time. Set in the circus, the film develops the story of a marriage between Sergei Sinitsyn, a clown of the state circus, and Olesia Batterbardt, the daughter of an academic, who is under the firm control of her mother, Malva Nikolayevna. Olesia still lives with her parents in a house on the outskirts of Moscow, which is decorated like a museum of modern art with numerous abstract paintings hung on the walls. At the beginning of the film Sergei visits an orphanage to take another look at the boy Vania, whom the couple will adopt the next day, since Olesia cannot have children. Back in the circus, he and his partner Roman, played by Vladimir Ilyin,[2] prepare a new number with a lion cage. Sergei's ex-girlfriend, the acrobat Polina, still worries about him and loves him. Olesia leaves with her father on a trip to Canada, surrendering to her parents' attempt to split up the 'unsuitable' marriage with a clown and prevent the adoption. However, Sergei picks up the boy from the orphanage. Together with Roman and his wife Alice they look after the boy, until he falls ill on the eve of an international tour that would have taken the clowns to Canada. Vania needs a rare blood group transfusion and Polina comes to his rescue. When Vania wakes up from his fever, he identifies Polina as his new mother.

The film, with comic elements in the circus scenes and melodrama around Vania and the relationship between Sergei, Polina and Olesia, raises several issues that are characteristic of Mikhalkov's work. First, the preoccupation with family background, in terms of the lack of moral standards, responsibility and a willingness to sacrifice in Olesia's Jewish intelligentsia family. The result is the impossibility of a marriage between the two 'classes' of the artist and the intellectual. On the other hand, there is the comradeship within the circus community: the director Dim Dimych is endowed with paternal features, ready to sacrifice a number to his competitor Fokine for the sake of enabling Sergei to stay with his sick son. Roman is prepared, albeit reluctantly, to give up an international tour. Mikhalkov simplifies Sergei's situation to a black and white portrayal of the goodies and baddies in the film, with a happy ending for Sergei, rewarded for his commitment to the adoption by a reunion with his beloved Polina, who is a much more humane and caring character than Olesia. The film was immensely successful (even though Kushnerev was of little renown), mainly as a melodrama with a happy ending starring two extremely popular actors, Oleg Menshikov and Vladimir Ilyin.

Mikhalkov's acting in this period related also to the comic genre. Eldar Riazanov is a film-maker of popular genres and musical comedies. Mikhalkov appeared in his *A Railway Station for Two* [Vokzal dlia dvoikh, 1982] in a minor role (the main parts were played by Liudmila Gurchenko and Oleg Basilashvili) as the conductor Andrei. Yet, even in this minor role, Mikhalkov dominated the entire film, while spatially he remained in control of the railway station. When he arrives his girlfriend Vera, a waitress in the restaurant, immediately walks up to him. He knows the station and everybody who works there, which makes it easy for him to do some illegal trading with melons. He is, of course, a womaniser, who does not take 'no' for an answer. Only the departure of the train is a reason for him to leave. When, in his second appearance, he finds that Vera is betraying him, he beats up his rival, yet has the politeness and manners of a gentleman to apologise and leave money in compensation for the damage done. Riazanov's *A Cruel Romance* [Zhestokii romans, 1984] is based on Alexander Ostrovsky's play *Without a Dowry* [Bespridannitsa, 1878]. The film scrupulously follows the play, in which the dowerless Larisa becomes the object of desire of four men in the provincial town: the married banker Knurov, the rich Vozhevatov, the poor civil servant Karandyshev and the dashing Paratov – played by Mikhalkov. Larisa loves Paratov, but he has to leave when he gets into financial trouble. When he returns to sell his Volga steamer 'Lastochka' (Swallow) Larisa has agreed to marry Karandyshev, who humiliates her at every step by regarding her as a symbol of his achievement. Larisa elopes with Paratov, Knurov and Vozhevatov. She spends the night with Paratov, who confesses that he is engaged to a rich woman who will save his fortune; Vozhevatov and Knurov throw a coin to decide who of them will take Larisa to Paris. Having become a mere object, Larisa no longer sees a meaning in life, and when she repeatedly refuses Karandyshev he shoots her in a fit of despair at her rejection. Mikhalkov's Paratov is a man who enjoys life, who is never depressed by his financial troubles, but who finds a way of solving his problems – selling his steamer without regret and marrying a rich woman out of sheer calculation.

Paratov has an exciting life to remember, and has no qualms about his action. He lives on the spur of the moment, accompanied by a gypsy band on his second visit. Paratov is no traitor, but he is prepared to ruin Larisa's reputation to get what he wants: pleasure. In this sense, the part of the hedonist Paratov offers more scope for an exploration of the joys of life that imbue the training of a Shchukin School actor.

Mikhalkov thus demonstrates here an interest in the comic genre; his characters dwell not on principles (Sinitsyn's unrequited love for Olesia, Paratov's refusal of the poor but charming Larisa) but on expediency and convenience. Mikhalkov also shows the first signs of an attitude of 'making the best of life', in a compromise after the appeal to act (*At Home Among Strangers*) and the challenge of the intelligentsia (*Slave of Love*) have failed.

Kinfolk

With *Kinfolk* Mikhalkov shifts to the present and creates a film about Moscow, in answer to Menshov's *Moscow Does Not Believe in Tears* [1980]. Menshov's melodrama extended over 20 years of Soviet life, from the 1950s to the 1970s, following the lives of three girls: Katia, Liuda and Tonia. Tonia marries Nikolai and lives in the countryside, leading a happy, rural lifestyle, but she remains absorbed in domestic problems without ever taking on a role in society at large. Liuda wants to secure her future not by her own career but by an advantageous marriage, but her husband, an internationally recognised ice hockey player, is an alcoholic. Finally Katia follows her path of making a sound contribution to society: she learns hard and becomes a factory worker; she works even harder and becomes a factory manager. Yet her private life remains hapless: she is a single mother. Her reward of happiness comes with a chance encounter with Gosha, who – after some hurdles have been overcome – assumes the role of the 'patriarch' of the family. The film was extremely popular at home and abroad because of its honest portrayal of Soviet life, exposing problems such as single motherhood and alcoholism without, however, drawing a bleak picture of contemporary life. The heroines were not modelled on the socialist ideal of women, but they all had their flaws and problems. It was this realism rather than the varnished version of Soviet life that dominated films of the 1980s, that made the film a blockbuster.

Kinfolk begins in the countryside and ends in the capital: from the point of view of movement the film completes the standard journey of Stalinist cinema, enhancing the significance of the capital. Yet there are subtle differences in Mikhalkov's view of the city. The film centres on the generational conflict, the theme of family relations and their role in modern society, and offers a comment on the loss of moral values in modern civilisation.

The film opens with a shot of provincial life as a man on horseback rides along the railway track and a train steams across the frame in the opposite direction. In the opening shot Mikhalkov immediately juxtaposes rural and urban lifestyles in two methods of travelling: horse and train. The camera pans on the station of Elan (the same place name as the village where Konchalovsky's *Siberiade* is set) and closes up on the cursing, crying and whining figure of a woman, Maria Vasilievna Konovalova, played by Nonna Mordiukova.[3] The casting for this part is crucial: Mordiukova epitomises the overpowering and dominant Soviet mother figure. Loaded with several heavy bags, Maria wants to travel to Moscow but cannot get a ticket. She sports a peasant kerchief that covers her fresh perm, a T-shirt with the Olympics logo, and a yellow jacket, all of which reflect her lack of fashion combined with a desire to follow the latest trend – characteristic of a provincial woman travelling to the capital. On the station square a man checks the details on his ticket, and she learns that he is travelling in a sleeping car on the next train, which is (as first-class accommodation) somewhat more expensive than a standard ticket.

Maria clearly manages to purchase a similar ticket: she is next seen on the train, sharing a compartment with the same gentleman. After Soviet pop music on the station, a classical aria now accompanies her into the carriage, a luxurious two-berth compartment – the pride of Soviet rail travel. Maria makes the acquaintance of her fellow traveller, Yuri Nikolayevich – a good-natured and Chaplinesque figure, created by Andrei Petrov. This encounter mainly serves the purpose of underpinning Maria's old-fashioned moral standards. She abhors the idea of sharing a compartment with a man and is about to leave the train when the conductor explains to her that it is common practice to have mixed occupancy in compartments; she returns to her seat. Yuri Nikolayevich, clearly an experienced traveller, invites her to share his tea with him and makes her feel comfortable without ever being patronising. Maria behaves like a child: when the train enters a tunnel, she screams; and she is tipsy after a sip of wine. Yuri Nikolayevich is a functional character, who serves as an opposite part to provincial life in the film's juxtaposition of urban and rural worlds. He allows the viewer to assess Maria Vasilievna's inexperience in travelling and her provincial background against the backdrop of an experienced traveller from Moscow. Subsequently, Yuri Nikolayevich develops as a character and his role increases in significance, although not in essence: he remains a litmus paper for Maria, never becoming a fully-fledged character.

Once the train has arrived in Moscow, Maria is met by her daughter Nina. Yuri Nikolayevich is met by a chauffeur, and so is another fellow traveller, the general, who will make several marginal appearances later in the film.

Maria's daughter Nina (Svetlana Kriuchkova) immediately strikes the viewer as an emancipated city dweller. She has advanced her career, having studied hard in order to move from the village into the capital. She is dressed in business style, sporting a raincoat and glasses to make her look more urban; she wears trousers, which Maria does not deem suitable for a woman; and she smokes, which causes the first in a series of arguments with her mother. Maria is further upset when she learns that Nina has separated from her husband. Maria believes in old family values, but she is confronted with a breakdown of those values around her: Nina has an affair, and Nina's daughter Irina shuts herself off from the constant remarks she gets from adults. Irina dresses up (like her mother) and dances to loud music when her mother and grandmother argue; she is addicted to the television and switches it back on several times even though her mother had turned it off. Irina is left to her own devices; with the ongoing arguments between her parents that must have preceded the departure of Irina's husband Stasik, and the current quibbles between Maria and Nina, Irina lives in her little world of love, not fight. She is driven into her own world of illusions by the lack of attention from her mother. Irina puts on a headset to listen to Boney M's track 'Sunny', living in her own world of foreign music and cutting out the lullaby her grandmother sings for her to send her to sleep.[4] Nina wears make-up and a Japanese kimono, and is hooked on fashion and appearance rather than her daughter's

9. *Kinfolk*, Yuri Nikolayevich (Andrei Petrov) and Maria (Nonna Mordiukova)

Modern Times: 1980–1985   73

education. She considers Irina's behaviour as 'normal' and symptomatic of modern urban children. Maria does not agree. Yet she follows their lack of manners and style: in the next scene she sports the same kimono with a Japanese emblem on the back that her daughter wore, and an apron with the stars and stripes of the American flag. Nina tells Irina off for dipping the spoon into the jar with the jam, and does the same a minute later. But Maria too, always concerned with manners and traditions, runs after her daughter with a spoon of pickles for her to try. Behaviour – bad or good manners – is repeated, and herein lies the 'kinship' of the title.

The spatial constraint in Nina's flat, occupied by three generations, is contrasted with the wide cityscape: the balcony of the suburban high-rise block of flats offers a view of Moscow, including the large and empty Olympic arena, where a lone runner exercises. A number of interpretations are possible here, such as loneliness or isolation in the big city, while the sequence also comments on the boycott (the absence of other runners) of the Olympics by America and 45 other countries in response to the Soviet invasion of Afghanistan.

Maria is next confronted with the external factors of life in the city: her daughter's ex-husband Stasik (Yuri Bogatyrev) comes to collect a few private things, and Maria hits him in the face for abandoning his family. Maria meets Yuri Nikolayevich in the park of the River Station (the docking point for ships cruising on the river Moskva); he awaits her with flowers and a new hat, which she rejects as 'unsuitably romantic', although she does wear the hat for the remainder of the day. Coincidences occur when they see the general on a boat, they lift weights, and have their photograph taken. All of these activities have comic results. After they have left the weight-pushing bar, a heavyweight person pushes the weight to the maximum level; the photo machine produces an image of Mikhalkov, Lebeshev and Adabashian instead of a picture of Maria and Yuri, hinting at the breakdown of technology. The radio announces runner no. 7 as Anatoli Pashvykin, who worked as set photographer on the film. After a series of arguments with Nina, Maria leaves the flat. The camera pans over the sky, where a military aircraft is seen taking off and usurping the entire screen – a further hint at the military action taking place in connection with the Afghan war.

Yuri Nikolayevich meets Maria at the train station and tries to help her with a hotel, but fails. While they sit in the lobby he tells her the story of his life; he missed his own wedding because he went on a boat trip with his mates. It transpires that Yuri Nikolayevich does not function simply as the prospect of an alternative life for Maria, but through the narration of his past he galvanises her to leap forward in order to sort out her own past. Maria is incapable of living in the present, and can address problems only if they have long been solved (or not) by others. In her spontaneous rush to put things 'right' Maria first sees her ex-husband, Vladimir Konovalov (Ivan Bortnik). She finds him in the barracks, leading a life centred on alcohol, allegedly working as an accountant. He acts as a clown for everybody, but is happy in his independence. He never wanted to be the chief engineer that Maria wanted him to be. More and more Maria emerges as a character who pushes people into doing what she believes to be good and right, without realising the destructive effect of her actions. Maria meddles in everybody's life, meaning well in all her interference but unaware that her concept of right and wrong may not correspond to that of the surrounding world.

Having had no success in convincing Konovalov of the worth of her lifestyle and value system, Maria visits Konovalov's second wife, who is not at home. Instead she speaks with his son Kirill (an early role for Oleg Menshikov), who is about to be drafted into the army. She tries to make him take responsibility for Konovalov's descent into alcoholism, not considering that he may be happy with the way he lives. Having failed here as well, she begs Stasik for forgiveness and asks him to return to Nina, while he is dating a young woman. She pursues them to a restaurant, where a wedding takes place. During the wedding party Stasik gives in and dances with her, driving her out of the restaurant by his overpowering movement. As Maria leaves the restaurant, army trucks are seen to be leaving Moscow. For the third time a subtle reference to a taboo theme of 1980 is made by commenting on the dispatch of young recruits to Afghanistan.

In the final part of the film – if we follow the division by the three references to Afghanistan: the runner, the aircraft, the trucks[5] – Maria says farewell to Yuri Nikolayevich, who has shaven off his moustache to please her. She leaves him, a lost and disconcerted man, in front of a metro station, declaring that she will return with her husband to the village. At the railway station she waits in vain for Konovalov, who has no desire to return to the provinces for what she believes is a better life for him. Maria never thinks of what others may want but imposes her own will, though without meaning to do harm. Konovalov has adapted to life in the city, as have Nina and Irina. They are different now from what they used to be like, yet Maria clearly cannot and will not accept this.

Maria misses her train and waits in the train station. In the morning, crowds of people arrive to accompany the recruits on their train journey. Konovalov shows up, bidding farewell to his son Kirill, and for a moment he is united with his Moscow family. The departure of the soldiers is accompanied by 'Farewell to the Slavianka' ('Proshchanie Slavianki'), a melancholic military farewell tune. Konovalov brings Maria into the circle of his family, and here she realises that she has, in effect, destroyed that family unity. She leaves the platform and walks down the tracks as Nina and Irina catch up with her. The final shot of the film sees the three generations reunited, with a view of Moscow's suburbia from the distance (from a train leaving for the 'provinces'), although the characters return to Moscow. Mikhalkov here deploys his favourite device of disconnecting time and space: Maria is viewed from a distance while she remains in the city. The camera withdraws to the point of the beginning of the narrative, emphasising that things in the provinces do not change, that the provinces harbour permanent positive high moral values that cannot be corrupted by city life. '*Kinfolk* shows the pain and inner rage of the director at how we ourselves destroy our spiritual world, chasing after some nonsense, after illusions, fog, and dreams, which begin to form the meaning of our life.'[6]

The film addresses the theme of province and city. Moscow is represented in its modern suburban architecture, and its Stalinist features are manifest in some selected locations: the park of the River Station (*rechnoi vokzal*), the Constructivist building where Stasik works, the entrance pavilion to a metro station, and railway stations. The screen Moscow is not the old, charming Moscow of pre-Revolutionary times but a mixture of the modern mass architecture and Stalin's grandiose buildings, in no way enchanting. Instead Moscow attracts with its modern lifestyle, however many old values have to be shed in order to afford living there. In this sense, the eminence and attractiveness of Moscow so typical of Stalinist culture is clearly reflected in the film.

Yet the film is also concerned with the deconstruction of modern civilisation that dominates the metropolis. The city is oppressive: the noise of city life is exaggerated; classical music (Beethoven's 'Moonlight Sonata') is distorted electronically; motorbikes race around peaceful courtyards; machines for instant photographs mix up their output; train announcements are nonsensical ('the train due at 22.00 yesterday is due at 7.35 tomorrow' leaves the speaker in a timeless zone). Planes, players, televisions and other examples of technology disrupt life in the city; yet in the village, too, the loudspeaker on the station is used to announce that a dog has been left tied on the station square and should be collected immediately. The city is corrupt and chaotic: there is no hotel room to be found; no train ticket to leave the capital; no service in the restaurant; and women wear trousers and smoke. Moscow is a den of corruption and inefficiency, devoid of any moral values. 'In the film the director tries to explore the very serious problem of the rough intrusion of civilisation into life, the destruction by mass culture of the national multiplicity and national foundations.'[7]

The pace of life in the city and its superficiality reduce characters to absurd caricatures. Yuri Nikolayevich is a Chaplin-like figure, subordinated to the matriarchal and overpowering Maria without a chance of taking a lead role in their relationship, but good-hearted and well-meaning. Stasik is a muscular man, who cannot even make a single point to Maria despite his physical power: she punches him in the face. The waiters in the restaurant talk about violins and imported cigarettes – things they cannot normally afford – rather than about their job and service. The groom has a broken wrist. Lara, the girl whom Stasik is taking for a meal, wears glasses with thick lenses, yet still cannot quite see the food on her plate. Irina is played by a boy, Fedia Stukov. Mikhalkov responds to a city that is stylised and exaggerated to the point of being grotesque, which makes Maria's serious-minded defence of provincial values even more genuine when set against the falsity and superficiality of urban life. Mikhalkov praises that which is absent, though: rather than producing a eulogy of provincial life by setting the film in the provinces, he disjoints image from time and transposes the defence of values into the city.

Mikhalkov also explores the relationship between characters. The title sounds sarcastic when connected to the disintegration of family life portrayed in the film. Konovalova tries to turn time back, remembering an idealised and different past. Her manners speak of a different reality, as do the reactions of those she visits in the present. Mikhalkov presents a mosaic of views and opinions, recollections and reactions, which are assembled through a principle of montage rather than superimposed in layers.[8]

Mikhalkov employed the folk ensemble of Dmitri Pokrovsky with its polyphonic folk tunes for the final scene, covering the cacophony of the argument between Nina, Irina and Maria on the tracks. He juxtaposes the music accompanying their reunion with the artificial classical music of Verdi that is heard during the train journey, and with the modern pop music of Boney M ('Sunny') that is used diegetically for the scenes in Nina's apartment. Occasionally, a tune composed by Artemiev is used to underline a romantic or dramatic scene; these are mostly electronic versions of Verdi or Beethoven used for the romantic encounters in the compartment and the meeting in the park, or Maria's departure, her despair after the scene in the restaurant, and her farewell to Yuri Nikolayevich. Mikhalkov again uses classical Western music as artificial, and folk tunes for genuine scenes, when Maria tries to remedy the intrusion of modern civilisation into the lives of her kinsfolk.

The film is bold in its references to the war in Afghanistan, especially the last scene of the railway station. Mikhalkov mentions in his film *Anna from Six to Eighteen* that some scenes were banned and the release of the film delayed for two years. It is one of the very few hidden references to politics, but serves also to highlight the need for the three women to be happy: none of their family has to leave for the war, while Konovalov's Kirill is drafted. The threat of war (a recurrent theme in Mikhalkov's films) ultimately unites Maria, Irina and Nina. As with the casting of Tabakov for the part of Oblomov,

Mikhalkov wins sympathy for Konovalova by casting Nonna Mordiukova to signal that she is right and civilisation wrong, even if things are moving towards progress. Mikhalkov condemns the loss of moral values in Russia, and this outright condemnation rather than the ambivalence of his earlier films made these films controversial or neglected in criticism.

Moscow Does Not Believe in Tears had over 80 million viewers, compared to 15 million for *Kinfolk*. *Kinfolk*, was released in 1982, but not shown at any international festival; it was quite popular in Russia, especially when compared to *Oblomov*. Mikhalkov here begins to dismantle Soviet life and point out the evil effects of civilisation. This is a theme continued in *Urga*, but more immediately in *Private Conversation*, where he also explores the moral corruption of a Muscovite.

Private Conversation

This film is based on a play for two actors, *A Conversation without Witnesses* [Beseda bez svidetelei, first published in *Teatr* 9 (1981)] by Sofia Prokofieva, exploring a meeting between two people who were once married. The play is open-ended, offering no solution to the situation. Mikhalkov had begun to rehearse the play at the Vakhtangov Theatre, Moscow, before he decided to abandon the theatrical production in favour of a film version. He had rehearsed with two of Moscow's best theatre actors so as to meet the need for a psychological portrayal of the characters – Irina Kupchenko and Mikhail Ulianov,[9] both engaged at the Vakhtangov Theatre. They also star in the film.

The origin of the film explains the static setting of the action in a flat. Frequently information is given through flashbacks or close-ups of a face in a spotlight as characters utter their thoughts, seemingly speaking to the audience. While not moving the setting of the play, Mikhalkov uses no innovative cinematic devices but explores a host of theatrical approaches. The woman ('She') watches on television a concert of Gluck's *Orpheus and Eurydice*, an opera commenting on the theme of love and sacrifice. She provides a narrative on the events as she is writing a letter to her new husband, Valentin Shliakhov.

A man ('He') enters the flat with his own key: he is no stranger. He is her ex-husband, and father of their son, Dima. During their argument it emerges that Dima is not her child but his son from a previous relationship, whom she cares for as if he were her own child. She devotes her love and attention to him, which is made visible by the abundance of trinkets and gadgets in Dima's room, when contrasted with the sparse decoration of the living room. 'He' is now married to the daughter of an influential professor, thus achieving social recognition and promotion. He is proud of his daughter by his second marriage, who plays in concerts, while caring little about his son Dima. In order to advance his career He has written a letter of denunciation of Valentin and, when He learns that She will marry Valentin, He fears revenge and repercussions. Moreover, his career and advancement on the social ladder are more important than his ex-wife's, or his own, personal happiness. His marriage seems to be unhappy, which accounts for his half-hearted attempt to make a pass at his ex-wife.

The tension rises gradually: He makes himself at home without asking, yet She does not take this as a provocation. He then begins to drink and tries to seduce her, which scares her a little, yet She remains in control of the situation. When He learns about her engagement to Valentin He becomes scared and increases his pressure on her: He threatens to take his son away from her. Given the choice between Valentin and Dima, She gives priority to her responsibility as a mother. He assumes that She is lying about her future marriage, convinced of his monopoly on happiness, and forces her to reject Valentin there and then, on the phone. When He realises that She is telling the truth, and that their son is actually doing his homework at Valentin's house, He feels the ground slipping under his feet and resorts to physical violence: He disconnects the phone and locks her in a cupboard. Throughout, He is the aggressor, while She reacts and responds only to his actions, following a typical male-female role division.

Ulianov has no motivation for his behaviour in the first part of the film: the reason for his visit is given only when He enquires about her new husband, Valentin, revealing the purpose of his visit together with his worry about the denunciation, of which She had no knowledge. His visit is thus in vain, yet He has now given away his reason and needs to make sure that She will not hamper his career by telling Valentin about the past. The past is the driving force for the present action, in which Ulianov creates for himself a series of roles, of husband, lover, career man, which are all nothing but a façade, and in the end He is punished for his insincerity by being driven into alcoholism.

However, morally, She is superior; Kupchenko plays the upright, fine, and intelligent character, while Ulianov, traditionally a positive hero, here creates a nasty perpetrator of abuse. They offer a crass division of good and evil, almost like a morality play. Their moral positions have no point of intersection; there is no gradation in the shades.

The film offers a circle to the narrative: She writes a letter from the future (happily married with a daughter), thus turning the events of that evening into the past. Mikhalkov relates events in a temporal distortion. Mikhalkov is not ambivalent in his attitude here, clearly siding with the woman who has sacrificed her life for her husband and his son, and who deserves her present happiness. Yet, in a narrative about present happiness and past nightmares the longing is not for a space or a time but for justice. Mikhalkov moralises in this film, which received few reviews, and those largely in literary, rather than cinematic journals.

The film is both within the mainstream and outside it at the same time. It fits into the range of works exposing the moral corruption of Soviet officials while rewarding those who suffered at their hands that was popular during the Thaw. Yet it contradicts the ethos of cinematic developments of the time, withdrawing into a theatrical space when the Soviet film industry engaged in bigger-scale projects, relying on special effects, popular genre and location for appeal to the audience, rather than in the acting skills of two actors. The individual career and personal happiness are pertinent themes of 1970s cinema, as encountered also in *Moscow Does Not Believe in Tears*, where personal happiness was the reward for social commitment. Here, personal happiness is the reward for truth, and in her case for her sacrifice of bringing up another woman's child as her own. Her sacrifice is rewarded not only by a new and happy marriage but also by her own daughter, as emerges from the letter She is writing to her new husband and finishing at the end of the film. While the play was open-ended, the film offers a romantic ending, rewarding moral values and never challenging the past by raising the issue of why she waited for nine years before marrying the man she loves.

10. *Private Conversation*, Ulianov and Kupchenko

The film also exposes the corruption, lies and denunciations that He engaged in for the sake of his career, not unlike Timofeyev in *Five Evenings*, who did not risk speaking the truth in order to safeguard his career. For Mikhalkov the men who spoke the truth (such as Ilyin) and who were victims of denunciation (such as Valentin) deserve happiness in their personal lives, even if their living conditions may be hard. Material suffering goes hand in hand with personal happiness, as is implicit also in orthodox faith, where the suffering on earth is believed to be rewarded after death. According to this equation a rich and successful man cannot be happy as well. She achieves happiness, ultimately, not because of a social contribution but because of her sacrifice. This attitude places the film not in the socialist tradition followed by Menshov but within a conservative and orthodox tradition that dwells on the concepts represented in the 'Russian idea', in the notion of sacrifice and reward after suffering. This casts a different light on the change to the ending: the idea is not so much to romanticise as to offer a reward.

The theme of family relations and the complexities of everyday life link the film to *Kinfolk*. Both films are set in urban flats, and here the restricted space of the flat is narrowed down even further when She is locked in the cupboard. In terms of design both films choose typically Soviet flats, with standard Soviet furniture and very little individual touch. Dima's room is representative of the young generation, and, like Irina, he is also influenced by Western rock music. But, like Slava in *Five Evenings*, he is studying hard, doing his homework with Valeri. *Private Conversation* – for all its theatricality – won a FIPRESCI award at the XIII Moscow International Film Festival in 1983, and received much critical appraisal for the acting of Ulianov and Kupchenko.

In these two films the role of women in Mikhalkov's work is crystallised. In *Slave of Love* and *Oblomov* they are beautiful, with elegant manners and exquisite taste. Elena Solovei provided all these qualities in both her Olgas (Voznesenskaya and Ilyinskaya). In *Mechanical Piano* Mikhalkov added another type of woman to his repertoire: the caring, loving, naïve and uneducated Sashenka, who is not spoilt by education and civilisation, as are the beautiful but devious Anna Petrovna, or the charming but shallow Sofia Egorovna. In the twentieth century women are not beautiful, but their charms lie elsewhere: Tamara is an old spinster, Zoya is superficial and shallow, but both are goodhearted. There is never any love in the present. Western influences turn women into objects of desire (Zoya) or into artificial, stylised puppets with mannerisms (Olga Voznesenskaya and Olga Ilyinskaya), while peasant and orthodox traditions produce a positive type of woman (Tamara, Maria and She). They are not necessarily distinguished by youth and outward beauty, but are mature and energetic, and they harbour Russian values (such as faith, happiness and a capacity for self-sacrifice).

5. Between East and West: 1985–1991

Gorbachev's reforms of glasnost and perestroika began first and foremost in the cultural sector, where liberals replaced hard liners: Egor Ligachev took the place of Mikhail Zimianin as Secretary for Ideology in the Central Committee of the Communist Party and Alexander Yakovlev took over the Agitprop Department. A convinced communist, Gorbachev assumed he could win over the masses by an appeal for their support through the medium of art, and to this end he invited the intelligentsia to Kremlin meetings to encourage the process of liberalisation. From 1987 onwards theatres and other cultural organisations were allowed budget freedom (*khozraschet*); theatre studios were legalised; the artistic unions were transformed through new leadership; rock concerts were allowed and became widespread; and, gradually, novels that had previously been published only in the West appeared in Soviet journals. The FU elected Elem Klimov as chairman, voting for a man whose films had suffered at the hands of censorship rather than the 'establishment' candidate, Mikhalkov. Subsequently, numerous films that had been shelved since the 1960s were released.[1] In 1987 the physicist and dissident Andrei Sakharov was allowed to return to Moscow after seven years under house arrest and internal exile in Gorky.

In terms of politics the Soviet Union opened up to the West. Gorbachev undertook numerous visits to Western countries, and, in an attempt to give the hierarchical Soviet party and state system a more democratic air, he created for his own office the title 'President' in 1988 and called for elections to a Congress of People's Deputies in 1989. Economically, joint ventures and co-productions with Western countries not only became possible but were encouraged.

By 1989 the liberalisation was clearly going farther and faster than Gorbachev had anticipated. In October and November of that year East

Germans sought refuge in Western embassies in Prague and Budapest, demanding asylum in the West. Throughout the German Democratic Republic there were silent protests against the Honecker regime. On 9 November 1989 the Berlin Wall 'fell' when people crossed the border at several checkpoints between East and West. By 1990 Germany was reunited. The 'Velvet Revolution' in Czechoslovakia brought in a democratic government, and the former dissident Václav Havel became president. In 1991 Boris Yeltsin was elected president of the Russian Federation – the first president within one of the constituent Soviet republics to be elected by the people. In August 1991 he led the opposition to a coup attempt staged by communist hard liners, who placed Gorbachev under house arrest in the Crimea and tried to assume power in order to return communist rule to the country. By the end of 1991 most Soviet republics had declared independence and the USSR was disbanded. Gorbachev resigned and Yeltsin remained president of the Russian Federation, formerly a constituent republic of the Soviet Union and now a state in its own right.

It is against this backdrop of events that Mikhalkov made the three films discussed in this chapter, all of which were co-productions with the West. In his early films Mikhalkov had sought to return the spirit of the Revolution to the present; then he had turned to nineteenth-century Russia to challenge, albeit indirectly, the stagnation, the entropy and lethargy of contemporary society. In the early 1980s he had expressed dissatisfaction with modern society which was losing sight of moral values. Having condemned his own contemporaries, he chose to look at Russia from the point of view of the West in his next films. This move to a more distanced perspective, combined with his longing for a Russia that no longer existed and that he sought to rebuild, formed the foundation for the 'Utopian nostalgia' that, from now on, dominated Mikhalkov's pining for a 'home' and his attempts to define 'his' Russia. In the films discussed here Mikhalkov creates a myth of Russia that is based not on authentic traditions but on invented and imagined stereotypes, turning this image of Russia into kitsch.[2] Citing Danilo Kis, Svetlana Boym has commented on the affinity between nationalist nostalgia and kitsch through representation that excludes a sense of humour and irony.[3] I interpret the three films of this period in the light of the view on national identity and Russia's spiritual values that Mikhalkov offers.

Dark Eyes

After having worked at Mosfilm since 1974, Mikhalkov left the studio in 1982 and formed his studio, TriTe. By the mid-1980s Mikhalkov's reputation as a film-maker had grown not only within Russia but also internationally, with the much-acclaimed *Mechanical Piano*. At a time when Tarkovsky was already filming in Italy, Mikhalkov was an obvious choice as a director for a co-production. In 1986 he was invited to Italy to direct a film based on Chekhov's story 'Lady with a Lapdog' [Dama s sobachkoi], which would feature Marcello Mastroianni in the main part of Romano. The film takes the title from a gypsy romance and transports the 'Lady with a Lapdog' to Italy. We see Italy through the eyes of the disillusioned Romano, who has become obsessed with Russia as a place of happiness. Yet his longing is for a space created through illusions, as Romano sees in Russia only what he wishes to see and what Russia wants to show of itself. Through his choice of Romano as a narrator, Mikhalkov lays the foundation for the creation of a non-authentic view of Russia's past, which Gillo Dorfles defines as 'kitsch'.[4]

In *Dark Eyes* Mikhalkov uses several themes from Chekhov's stories and turns them into a melodrama. Mikhalkov largely draws on 'Lady with a Lapdog', but complements his adaptation with scenes, themes and characters from other Chekhov stories: Romano's family life is drawn from 'The Name-Day' [Imeniny], where the husband of the story's heroine cares little for her until it is too late; Anna's family life bears parallels to that of Anna in 'Lady with a Lapdog', but her relation with her husband, who sees her merely as an object of pride, echoes 'Anna round the Neck' [Anna na shee].

The film begins with scenes of Romano at his Italian home; Elisa, the only child of a rich family, married Romano, the son of a poor shopkeeper, against her parents' will. Once the couple settled into their comfortable life, their love waned and life became a routine. When Elisa encounters financial problems, Romano leaves for the spa Montecatini Terme. There he meets Anna, and they spend the night together, but by the morning Anna has left. A vulgar matron of the hotel hands over a letter, written in Russian. Romano returns to Rome and has the letter translated at the university, lying about the addressee. Anna declares in the letter that she fled from love. As Romano can elicit no emotional response from Elisa, he believes that he reciprocates Anna's love and finds a pretext to go to Russia: to sell the unbreakable glass his brother-in-law has invented. Romano finds Anna in a provincial town; she is the wife of the mayor, Modest Petrovich. Anna takes refuge in prayer when she realises Romano has come, but he nevertheless disturbs her peace. He promises to arrange for her to join him in Italy. Upon his return to Italy he finds that he is bankrupt; Elisa is selling the house, having been cheated by her lawyer. She has found Anna's letter and now confronts Romano, who renounces his love, failing once again to speak the truth and instead playing a record with Russian music. In the civilised society of the West the artistic reproduction of the original Russian music (with the whole lifestyle that goes with it) is the only thing that remains. After eight years have passed, and with

Romano now earning a living as a waiter, he concludes that there never was any love between him and Anna. Here the visitor and Romano's interlocutor, Alexeyev, kicks in with the story of his wife, Anna: he saved the unhappy woman after she had left her husband to follow the man she loved; she became suicidal and an alcoholic when she realised that this man (Romano) did not love her. Alexeyev knows there is no love in their relationship, but Anna is loyal to him.

While in Chekhov's 'Lady with a Lapdog' there is an open ending in the relationship between Gurov and Anna, and the plot develops between the spa of Yalta, the provinces and Moscow, Romano (as the Italian version of Gurov) displays less commitment to their relationship, but also a longing for the impossible reunion of Russia and Italy, East and West. In Mikhalkov's version Anna is a victim of a male-dominated society, and not, as in Chekhov, a woman capable of breaking free from an unhappy marriage.

It is worth comparing Mikhalkov's film with an earlier film version of the story, Kheifits's *Lady with a Lapdog* [Dama s sobachkoi, 1960]. Kheifits's film demonstrates fidelity to the original, which it follows meticulously, and endows the background with the social ills of the time, exposing poverty and offering a critique of Russia in the late nineteenth century that is much in line with socialist values. It is a critical view of Russian society as a redundant world, destined and doomed to be replaced by the new socialist Russia in the twentieth century. Mikhalkov clearly departs from this view, idealising the Russia of the late 1890s as a place of idleness but no social hardship. Even the vagrant life of the gypsies and the stifled life of Anna in the provincial town are glossed over. Mikhalkov creates a myth of the life of provincial Russia in the late nineteenth century, ignoring the encroaching hardship on the middle classes that was perceived in *Mechanical Piano* (the servant's refusal to obey, the reports of women working in the fields, the bankruptcy of the estate). There is neither critique nor irony in the portrayal of Russia in *Dark Eyes*, which is therefore mythogogic.[5] The Kheifits film adaptation treats Chekhov in the conventional and conservative Soviet way, seeking to explore the social injustice of imperial Russia.

Dark Eyes begins with a series of late nineteenth- to early twentieth-century cartoon-like drawings, seemingly from old newspapers (the paper has yellowed), showing scenes of people boarding a ship and the ship's departure on a sea voyage. The final cartoon is brought to life with Pavel Alexeyev peering through the window into the restaurant, where he sees Romano. Alexeyev enters and makes Romano's acquaintance, and they sit down at a table. The enclosed space of the restaurant makes the minds of Romano and Alexeyev wander as Romano reminisces about the past when he learns that Alexeyev is from Russia. A photo showing Elisa and her family is animated.

Romano shows Alexeyev photographs to illustrate the (unreliable) narrative of his own life, including his visit to Russia. Rather than hearing about Russia first-hand from a Russian visitor, Romano imposes his view of the country onto Alexeyev – a view that bears the imprint of a foreign gaze and is therefore non-authentic and thus doomed to be 'kitsch'. Romano narrates his life in a series of flashbacks, endowing the film with a subjective perspective. The photograph that triggers the narrative is a document of the past, of a real life, that becomes animated. Romano subsequently observes himself acting and performing a role. During the film the camera returns occasionally to the two men in the restaurant to remind us of the present. Alexeyev's short narrative at the end is not supported visually, while Romano's past has images. Yet Romano has no images of the present, while Alexeyev lives in the present. Mikhalkov teases the viewer into a complicated game with time and images, asserting the visually richer past (Romano) over a static and uninteresting present (Alexeyev).

Romano's story harks back to his marriage and his departure for Montecatini Terme when his wife Elisa encountered financial problems with her estate; the theme of *The Cherry Orchard* clearly resonates here, even if the Italian estate is lost due to betrayal rather than inactivity and Elisa manages the sale, facing up to the situation herself. The spa offers an outlet for repressed activities, encouraging the development of a carnivalesque atmosphere of playing roles and games. The patients dance in their wheelchairs to waltz music; they immerse themselves in mud baths; and Romano's former mistress Tina arrives to check on him. She claims to have come alone, without her husband Manlio, threatening to resume the affair with Romano and leading him to pretend that he is sick and cannot move his legs. In this exercise of masking and playing the Russian lady, Anna (with a dog) attracts Romano's attention. Romano invents an absurd story about his 'weak' legs (a hereditary condition that is linked to the Vesuvius eruption) and pretends to be cured by the Russian word *sobachka* ('little dog', or 'lapdog'). Yet, instead of making Romano an absurd failure *à la* Platonov, Mikhalkov endows him with a melancholy for Russia that has no foundation but that seems to lend a meaning to Romano's life that he lacks in Italy. Romano tells Anna a false and pitiful story of his life: he is a clown and pretender, never serious, but an excellent actor.

Romano follows Anna to Russia. Once in St Petersburg Romano sees one official after the other, all of whom fail to provide him with a travel permit to go to Sysoyev, afraid to make a decision that involves responsibility for a foreigner. One official has no ink, the other has his hands entangled in his sleeves, and only after a dance performance on the unbreakable glass does Romano get the permission signed. Again, performance and acting are rewarded. Alighting at Sysoyev, Romano finds himself in a field, while across the railway line an official reception awaits him: red carpet and brass band, bread and vodka. In this episode Mikhalkov pokes fun at Soviet officialdom and bureaucracy, and alludes to the prevailing superficiality and façade: the letter 'S' of the station name falls off as soon as the delegation has left; a fence collapses as workers try to fix it. Everything is a façade in 1880s Russia.

Romano is more at home in Russia than in Italy. The officials' fear of reaching a decision and the shunning of action (the factory for Sysoyev) are characteristics that Romano shares with the Russians; he has escaped from solving problems and selling family property in Italy. Similarly, the superficiality and façades prevailing in Russia correspond to Romano's acting skills. This façade, however, pretends that Russia belongs to European civilisation, while nature truly harbours Russia's spiritual values. It is noteworthy that most nature shots offer a view of a church, echoing the common practice of building churches on hills so that they would be visible from the surrounding settlements (the church should be seen from all the houses).

Mikhalkov draws a fine distinction between the style of the Italian villa with its rich interiors and its ascetic terracotta-colour exteriors, as opposed to the architectural opulence of the mansion in *Mechanical Piano*. The Italian villa offers spacious interiors that provide coolness from the outside heat, and flights of rooms that separate characters. Montecatini Terme is flanked by white marble columns and floors, and all characters are correspondingly dressed in white, making these distinct Italian spaces. What is more stunning is the cardboard appearance of St Petersburg, with its empty streets and squares and flimsy façades, clearly shot in a studio and not on location. If Italy provides a lavish authentic setting, then St Petersburg is a flimsy cardboard decor for a cheap theatre.

The Mayor of Sysoyev sees potential investment with the arrival of a Western visitor and greets Romano accordingly. The local vet, Kostia, asks Romano not to build a factory here as it would destroy nature and demolish the landscape of the little town, located on a river. Mikhalkov's images of Italy capture the classical architecture of a Roman villa in the south of Italy, and Montecatini Terme. Yet Mikhalkov treats high culture with a degree of frivolity: the space of Elisa's house creates a separation between the couple; Romano plays the fool in the garden and is bored at the concert; the life at the spa is also stifled, and conversations are boring until Romano breaks free and performs. When in Russia Romano really enjoys himself in the general masquerade of life in Sysoyev and behind the façades of St Petersburg. Although in Italy Romano can break free of conventions, in Russia he joins the general carnival of life behind masks and façades. Therefore he feels more at home in Russia, without acknowledging that this is a performance space rather than an original for the foreign visitor.

When Romano is taken to the nearby station by the vet Kostia, they ride on a cart across the river and through a valley. Kostia, modelled on Chekhov's character Astrov (*Uncle Vania*), conducts a monologue about nature. Kostia echoes the perennial concern with nature in Chekhov's work, but also Mikhalkov's obsession with forests, fields and rivers. Romano dreams of his mother and remembers how he covered his ears with his hands when his grandma sang the lullaby 'Ninna Nonna' for him, while the gypsies ride past singing their songs. Indeed, the scene of Romano riding through the Russian countryside is accompanied only by the Italian lullaby and then by a gypsy song. Romano has regained his roots, and Russia is seen as a country that accommodates all nationalities (not unlike the lullaby sung in all languages of the Soviet empire at the end of Alexandrov's *The Circus* [Tsirk, 1936], when the multi-ethnic audience sings for the heroine's little black son, Jimmy, adopting him thereby into the Soviet community) and makes them feel at home. Romano believes that he has a Slavic soul and has more affinities with Russia than his native Italy. Mikhalkov offers two perspectives: the view on Italy seen through the eyes of a Russian director (himself), and the view on Russia seen through the Italian visitor. He also introduces two spaces of Russian life: the town and city, which are façade only, and the countryside, which is genuine.

11. *Dark Eyes*, Romano (Marcello Mastroianni) and the vet Kostia (Dmitri Zolotukhin) on the cart

After Romano's narrative has ended we return to reality: Romano must lay the tables in the restaurant; Alexeyev wakes up his wife. The sunset reflects in Anna's face, and the shot dissolves in the image of the Russian valley. The final image is that of a vast Russian field, the ultimate embodiment of the Russian soul with its quietude and width, with qualities that will never change in Mikhalkov's view. The images of space (cartoons of the ship) have turned into real space, in which more images of space are created in the characters' minds: the past is re-enacted in the form of a meta-film. Nature is filled with another meaning: the image of the Russian valley is frozen, representing Russia in the final shot. The valley, devoid of human life, is the absolute space of a past irretrievably lost for the individual but accessible to the entire nation as an artistic product created by Mikhalkov. In Gilles Deleuze's terms, Mikhalkov separates the virtual and real, never coalesces them, and thus never produces a 'crystal-image'; instead, he rejects the real and the virtual, and creates his own image.[6] Mikhalkov not only creates his own space called Russia, but also his own time: 'Mikhalkov wants to live in his own time. He has invented his own civil war, his own 1936, his own Goncharov, his own Chekhov.'[7]

Mikhalkov replaced the contrast between the Black Sea resort, Moscow and a provincial Russian town in the original story with the contrast between Italy and Russia, West and East. The Italian Romano experienced love, failed to recognise it and lost it, not caring for others. The Russian man Alexeyev has no love, but spends his life devoted to others. The Western man is incapable of real love, while the Russian man is capable of love and sacrifice. In the juxtaposition between Russia and Europe it is Russia that carries the moral triumph, leaving Europe a victim of its corrupt moral values and double standards. Romano is now a waiter in a restaurant, and lies to his boss about having met an old friend. Even in the present he cannot tell the truth, remaining a compulsive liar.

Both the music from Mozart's *The Barber of Seville* ('Una voce poco fà') which accompanies the meeting between Anna and Romano, and the location of the Russian provincial town (shot in Kostroma) anticipate themes of *The Barber of Siberia*, in which the confrontation between classical and popular, East and West, goes much further. While glorifying classical Western culture and heritage, Mikhalkov cherishes Russia. He is unable to resolve the conflict between classical and modern, and more importantly the clash between past and present. He varnishes the past (not the present, as Socialist Realism), and pines for a return to the past while rebuilding it to suit his own vision. Mikhalkov portrays the poor Western traveller, himself spiritually impoverished, who finds meaning in Russia, a country that can never be fully understood. Here, again, Mikhalkov anticipates the view presented in *The Barber of Siberia*: 'He is Russian, and that explains everything.'

Dark Eyes has received little critical attention in Russia. A review after the television screening of the film in 1994 comments on this fact, and Pavel Lebeshev remembers the House of Cinema audience leaving even during the screening.[8] The hostility to the film is also illustrated by the relative absence of reviews of the film in the major film journal (*Iskusstvo kino*) and other major newspapers with serious film columns. Instead, *Sovetskaia kultura* carried several readers' responses and short critical comments. The film was criticised for its profanation of Chekhov and the parody of Soviet bureaucracy, but the main accusation levelled at the film was the attempt to cater for Western audiences by producing a kitsch version of Chekhov.[9] The most outraged responses came from provincial readers (as if they were most qualified to comment on the portrayal of life in Sysoyev). A reader from Tallinn commented: 'It is good that our film-makers strive for collaboration with the West. But they do not notice that they are losing something very important. Neither the fine foreign film stock nor the foreign actors can replace that loss. Between *Mechanical Piano* and this film lies an enormous distance. In the first film, there is the high quality of the soul; in the second, the high quality of the film stock.'[10] The reader Lepshei from Minsk continued: 'Why does he [Mikhalkov] consider the most typical traits of the Russian character... to lie in the basic lack of culture, in the drunkenness to a level of loathing, in the humiliating ingratiation before foreigners. [...] How beggarly and primitive is Mother Russia! You can only "drink bottoms up", and dance, intoxicated, to gypsy songs.'[11] But also Nina Agisheva, reporting from the Cannes festival, writes: 'In this film Russia is seen through the eyes of an Italian in the literal [...] and figurative sense. For a foreigner Russia is frequently associated just with gypsies, black caviar, vodka and illogical and inexplicable ways of life.'[12]

Dark Eyes was nominated for an Oscar, and was entered in the competition programme of the 1987 Cannes Film Festival, where Mastroianni won the Best Actor award. It was the first Russian film in several years to be entered into the competition programme of this most prestigious film festival of the world (in the 1980s only Tarkovsky and the Georgian film-makers Lana Gogoberidze and Tengiz Abuladze had films in the Cannes competition). There was, therefore, a degree of envy from Russian critics, especially after the success that Tarkovsky had experienced at Cannes and that they seemingly wished to see unchallenged, and possibly also to do with the co-competitor, *Repentance*, a clearly much more important film for Soviet audiences in 1986/87.

Both *Dark Eyes* and Tarkovsky's *Nostalgia* look at Russia from a distance, and both film-makers are dislocated from their homeland at the time of the film's making (and both intending to return at the time of filming). In *Nostalgia* approaches and conclusions are entirely different from *Dark Eyes*. In Andrei Tarkovsky's films Russia is rendered through the poetic image of a landscape with a country house (*Mirror*), or a meadow with a hut by a little pond where past and present merge (*Nostalgia*). In *Nostalgia* the wooden house is not only in the past but also in the distance, and it is simultaneously in the present and in Italy, surrounded by ruins. Tarkovsky's Gorchakov harbours values within himself, within his personal memory, that he transfers onto other times and spaces, aware of this in a reflective nostalgia. Tarkovsky transposes his image into the here and now, unifying the space of Italy and Russia while representing through this very same image the dichotomy of his character, split between Russia and Italy, past and present.[13] Romano longs for a country that was never his, trying to build for himself a different past that he feels closer to than the lullaby of his grandmother, a past that has no images. He betrays himself, not only restoring a past but building a past that he never belonged to, either in time or space. Romano falls in love with a woman he cannot understand, with a country that he cannot understand. He fails in the here and now because of his inability to realise that his 'longing' (*algia*) is based on a misunderstanding of the 'home' (*nostos*).

The Russia that Mikhalkov presents is a country seen through the eyes of a foreigner, who views superficially (he really is searching for Anna) and fails to look beyond the surface (literally, in the case of the unbreakable glass). On that surface he finds all his prejudices confirmed: petty bureaucrats who cannot or will not make decisions; beautiful façades; vodka-drinking people; young men obsessed with the environment; good-hearted people; and charming and cheerful gypsies. Clearly this view of Russia is cliché-ridden, and represents the impressions of a traveller who wants to have his preconceptions confirmed. As a Russian director Mikhalkov could have taken a different approach. Instead, he confirms to the West its romanticised and idealised view of nineteenth-century Russia. He presents a cheap print (*lubok*) of his own country as a space that is, as such, neither desirable nor within reach. Only its attributes (Anna's devotion, the gypsy's carefree lifestyle, the beauty of the countryside glorified visually and in the words of the vet) are desirable for Romano. He mistakes the part for the whole, and this illusion makes him a character dishonest with himself, despicable in his conduct, but lovable for the actor who plays him – Marcello Mastroianni. With *Dark Eyes* Mikhalkov moves the furthest away from the reflective or ironic nostalgia of his earlier films towards a restorative nostalgia that tends towards nationalistic revival.

Hitchhike

While in Italy Mikhalkov was commissioned to make a film sponsored by the car-makers Fiat, entitled *Russian Elegy* [1990]. He used the material for this film to make his own full-length feature film, *Hitchhike*, in the style of a road movie. It traces the journey of a driver, Sandro, from Italy to Russia, to a small village outside Moscow, in order to test-drive a Fiat car.

The film begins in Italy: Sandro is test-driving a car before informing his boss of his project to drive across Europe to Russia. Sandro, who has recently lost his wife, packs a case and sets off. At his first stop he visits a bar, where he picks up a good-looking woman, who stays with him for the night. The next morning he continues his drive after refuelling the car. He travels onward, through Poland, where he picks up a woman on the roadside and stays the night with her at her flat.

The road gets icy and snowy as he passes the border into Russia. He drives into Moscow, past the Central Telegraph, the Kremlin, along Kutuzov Avenue, and out into the countryside. On the roadside he offers a lift to a heavily pregnant woman (Nastia), who is in labour and on her way to the clinic. Her husband follows on a motorbike and, when he catches up with the car, Sandro stops, packs the bike into the boot and continues the drive. Sandro plays Italian opera music as the camera pans across the beautiful Russian landscape. Cultural values of high art are associated with Italy, with Western culture, while the feeling for nature is reserved for Russia.

As she is about to give birth Nastia leaves the car, followed by her husband who brings boiled water and clothes from Sandro's suitcase. She dares not soil the car while giving birth, yet she also wishes to be at one with Russian nature rather than a Western automobile, comfortable as this may be. The baby is born in the midst of the snowy Russian countryside, and then they drive to the hospital. Sandro goes to a telegraph office, where he no longer reacts to the female receptionist's flattery while waiting for a call. He calls his son, Lucca, and asks for forgiveness, saying he will come back. Outside children are playing around the car, and Sandro takes them for a ride. They look at the pictures of the Pope and Ornella Muti that Sandro has displayed on the front of his car, thinking these are Sandro's loved ones. Yet, while it is Russian practice to share images of loved ones openly, Sandro keeps the image of his son hidden in his jacket. Finally the car disappears over the horizon, giving way to the view of a horse standing in a field.

Sandro's visit to Russia enables him to find a meaning in life after the loss of his wife. Having witnessed the unity of man and nature at the birth of a child, he realises the importance of his son. Russia offers an experience that re-establishes lost values. In the West and en route, Sandro displayed the qualities of Western decadence: he is a playboy who picks up any woman on the roadside. In Russia he comes to his senses. The experience of Russian life enables Sandro to overcome his loss and realise the real value in life: children.

The car journey has no destination, so it is a journey of self-discovery through acquaintance with another culture. The plot is a little far-fetched and unconvincing, but it is interesting to see the trouble Mikhalkov took to emphasise the impact of Russian life and the Russian countryside on a foreign visitor. Mikhalkov glorifies the Russian fields, offering a rare view (in his films) of the Russian countryside in winter. However, the car serves – as in *Slave of Love* – as a cocoon: it is the space for Sandro's recognition of the real spiritual values, a space representing the West where the Russian woman does not even want to give birth. Mikhalkov creates a totalising myth, elevating Russia through clichéd spiritual values of 'Mother Russia' and nature. The film, promulgating Mikhalkov's myth of the Russian soul, received no substantial critical attention, and no theatrical release in the collapsing Russian film market of the early 1990s.

During this period of collaboration with the West Mikhalkov also participated in an international project in his capacity as actor. In *The Insulted and Injured* [Unizhennyie i oskorblennye, 1990], an adaptation of Dostoevsky's novel in a Swiss–Russian co-production directed by Andrei Eshpai Junior, Mikhalkov played Count Valkovsky, starring alongside Nastassia Kinski. The film, which heavily relies on the use of Ivan Petrovich as narrator, portrays the count as a person who always has the upper hand, who not once loses his self-confidence, even in the most delicate situations. Mikhalkov's Valkovsky first appears in Natalia Nikolayevna's barren flat, with a monologue in which he offers his son Alesha free choice of his future wife, having hitherto resisted the marriage to Natalia. He expects to be listened to, and not to be spoken with. He is further shown as a shadowy figure, observing Ivan Petrovich in the poor quarters of the city and visiting the house of an impoverished family. Finding that Alesha has not seen Natalia for a while, the count does not keep his promise to her: he accuses Alesha of neglecting Natalia, thereby driving him away from her into the arms of the rich Ekaterina Fedorovna, Valkovsky's bride-elect. Mikhalkov never lets Valkovsky appear a schemer. Even when he visits Ivan Petrovich and offers him money to marry Natalia, he turns this offer into a provocation when he sees Ivan Petrovich's reaction of disgust at such a move. Valkovsky is a puppeteer, with a great ability for improvisation, which allows him to turn any situation to his favour. He is abusive of people believing in ideals, classifying them as 'sick'. Mikhalkov's Valkovsky is patronising and charming at once, clearly remaining in control. His manoeuvres are rewarded when the financially beneficial marriage comes about, but his illegitimate daughter Nelli vows on her deathbed never to forgive Valkovsky for having neglected her after her mother's death. The character of Valkovsky echoes the characteristics of Mikhalkov as director in this period: the manoeuvring of things in the direction he wants them to go.

Urga

After the collapse of the Soviet Union and its film industry Mikhalkov activated his contacts in the West, having gained experience of foreign productions with *Dark Eyes*. By this time he had set up TriTe, which now co-produced *Urga* with Michel Seydoux and Camera One (France). *Urga* was shot in China with a native Mongolian cast and the actor Vladimir Gostiukhin in the part of Sergei. It explores the traditions of the Mongolians and juxtaposes oriental traditions to those of Western civilisation, thus developing Mikhalkov's view on the Eurasian issue (which views the role of Russia as a hybrid of European and Asian cultures), but also exploring the relationship between civilisation and ethnic lifestyles.

The opening shot offers a view of a rider on a white horse, from the back, the front and the side, standing in the open steppe before chasing another rider on a black horse. Both riders hold onto a long pole with a loop used for catching animals, the *urga*, before falling into the grass. Here the man tries to embrace the woman, who pushes him back and escapes into the distance, towards tent (*iurta*) and herd. As the sun sets the man and the woman, Gombo and Pagma, join up: Pagma refuses to make love to her husband since they have three children, and that is one too many already by Chinese law. The baby is rocked in the cradle by Gombo's mother; the six-year-old daughter Burma and her younger brother Buyin wait for their parents' attention; and Buyin has tied a red scarf to his father's *urga* as a playful reminder.

Throughout the film, the family is visited several times by their uncle, Bayartu, who is always drunk, has neither home nor family, and claims that Sylvester Stallone's Rambo, whom he shows on a poster, is his brother. He rides through the steppe with all his belongings – an umbrella and a suitcase. The family then represents a more stable, settled version of the Mongolian tribe than the nomadic uncle.

Gombo is a loving and caring father: he takes his little boy into the field and tells him a story about the wind that blew away the Mongolians' horses, about Genghis Khan and his horde. He catches a dragonfly to show the child how it makes music with its wings. In the meantime the women weave, and Pagma finds a toy in her sleeve, which Buyin has hidden there from his sister. The children are clearly loved by their parents, especially the little boy.

The idyll is disrupted when a truck runs across the fields with a driver, Sergei, who is falling asleep at the wheel. Even turning up Wagner's opera *Lohengrin* on the radio does not stop him from dozing off again. He wakes up abruptly at the loud finale of the aria, and manages to stop the van on the edge of a river. He gets out of the cabin, stretches his legs and runs through the steppe, where he stumbles over a dead body shredded by vultures. Scared out of his wits, he runs back to the truck to drive off, and puts it into the wrong gear: instead of reversing, he moves the truck over the edge and leaves it hanging over the embankment, with the front bonnet plunged into the water. His calls for help are heard by Gombo, who rides to the scene. He promises help the next day and takes Sergei back to his tent to offer him hospitality.

Sergei, a kind of Soviet popular prototype with his steel teeth, tattoos, poor speech and no manners, is horrified by the traditions of the Mongolian family. He is appalled that they leave the body of Gombo's brother in the fields to offer him rest, in line with Buddhist traditions; he asks for a telephone in the middle of the steppe; he is disgusted when Gombo, with the assistance of his children, slaughters a sheep; and he initially refuses to eat with the family in their tent, preferring his own sandwiches. When he joins them, he behaves in a way that suggests his assumed superiority. Only once he has had enough alcohol to drink, and once Burma plays a Russian folk song on her accordion, does he feel at home and fall asleep in the tent, snoring loudly.

In the morning Pagma explains to Gombo again the impossibility of making love and running the risk of another pregnancy. Instead, she sends him to town to buy condoms, which she – the city girl – has seen on television. Gombo goes to the nearby town with Sergei, loading his horse onto the truck. For the first time he tastes civilisation, in the form of sugar plums, roundabouts,

12. *Urga*, Gombo and Pagma playing with the 'urga'

bicycles and televisions. In the pharmacy, where he is eagerly offered condoms, he cannot bring himself to make the purchase.

Sergei meets his wife Marina: Sergei has to work far away from his native Irkutsk to earn money as a road construction worker. Their daughter finds no Russian-speaking children at school to play with. In an argument in a bar Sergei is reminded of his ancestors, who were killed during the war, and he asks the disco band to play 'On the Hills of Manchuria', a waltz about the defeat of the Russian army in the Russo–Japanese War that he has tattooed on his back. He is arrested by the police and bailed out by Gombo; Gombo may be a stranger in the city, but he will never let his friend down.

Gombo prepares his return home. On the way he wants to ask the lama about the use of condoms, but in the recommended prayer he finds no answer to his immediate question. Gombo continues his journey, having purchased a television and a bike. As he is resting in the field he has a vision of a horde of Mongolians approaching him, accusing him of a betrayal of values by purchasing a television and a bike, and taking him and Sergei hostage. Gombo is a Mongol, a descendant of Genghis Khan, himself a fourth child. Genghis Khan displays the attributes the Mongolian Gombo has had to compromise: he is the master of space (the steppe); the master of women (Pagma is in his horde); and the master of a large number of horses and their riders. The reflection of the horde on the blank television screen is turned into a Western-style movie extract.

When Gombo returns home, modern civilisation impacts on the family: the grandmother pierces the bubble paper of the television wrapping; the boy hides in the box for the television. Gombo connects the television to a wind machine and turns his *urga* into an aerial. The family watches television: first they see the meeting of Gorbachev and Reagan reported on American television, which slides over to Chinese television reports. Gombo claims that the condoms were sold out. Pagma leaves the tent, and then figures in the steppe image on the television screen; Gombo follows her. Their life in the steppe is as interesting as the television reports just seen. They ride off, and place the *urga* (the sign not to disturb a Mongolian couple in the steppe when making love) in the field.

The epilogue features a narration by Temujun, Pagma and Gombo's fourth child, who now works at the petroleum refinery, which with its tall chimneys dominates the site where the *urga* once stood, replicating the phallic shape of the urga. He is married but has no children yet. He has travelled to Irkutsk, where Russians used to live, and will visit Los Angeles and Japan in the future. The ringing of the telephone permeates the final titles of the film. In this dystopian vision, modern civilisation has destroyed the Mongolians' lifestyle on the outskirts of the Soviet empire. In this sense, the film comes down on the side of Eastern cultures, and Mikhalkov's frequently cited Russophilia has shifted to Asia. Certainly, Western influence and the destruction of the beautiful landscape of the steppe lie at the heart of the film, expressing an almost environmentalist concern.

> It seems to me that the author of *Urga* has gone further than the concept of the 'greens': he stands up for the ecology of the environment but also for the ecology of love. From the position of contemporary 'urban' man he wants to praise some of our ancestor's original ethics and aesthetics that are untroubled by the socium. Nikita tries to convince us (or himself?) that the life of Nature is 'pure' life.[14]

The epilogue is puzzling in its temporal reference: it could be assumed that the factory is the present, but in fact the television hints at the late 1980s setting for the main story, so that the epilogue would be 20 years later – i.e. in the first decade of the twenty-first century, when the child conceived in the late 1980s would have reached marrying age. Mikhalkov again blurs the notion of time, as seen earlier in his views of a permanent, unchanging Russian valley that embodies Russian values at all times and ages.

Mikhalkov returns to the lifestyle of the predecessors of Russia, finding them not in the Western Slavs but in the eastern tribes of the Mongolians. He thus clearly comes down on the Eastern, Asian side in his notion of Russia, not part of Europe but superior to Western civilisation. He makes a stab at Soviet features on the way in the figure of Sergei and the theme of industrialisation. 'To remind us of the roots Mikhalkov returns to the pre-root state. The ancestors are steppe people, in whose world even the native Russians, when entering the world circus, are Westerners no better than Rambo.'[15]

In the juxtaposition between Russia and the West Mikhalkov dwells on the superiority of Russia, with its people's readiness for sacrifice and selfless conduct, inspired by the grandeur and force of the Russian fields and rivers. In the juxtaposition of Russia and the East, Russia is enriched by Eastern traditions, which appear as an integral part of Russia even if they may seem strange to the Western visitor (both Sergei in *Urga* and Jane in *Barber*). 'According to Mikhalkov Russia does not need Westernisation, because it is itself an inseparable part of the West – of course, if you are looking from the East. Russia is a multicultural superpower of the 21st century.'[16] Both Gombo and Sergei are victims of civilisation: Gombo is restricted in his lifestyle with regard to the number of children the family is allowed to have, while Sergei is forced to work away from his native town. Both cultures are under threat: Sergei's child cannot find any other child to speak Russian with, and Gombo's lifestyle is extinct at the end of the film when the tent is replaced by a factory.

A major concern in all of Mikhalkov's films is the destruction of landscape, the distortion of the majestic beauty of the Russian motherland. In all three films discussed in this section Russia is glorified, while Mikhalkov's nationalist pride is disguised in the concern for landscape. In the 1990s, after the end of the Soviet era, Mikhalkov would be preoccupied more and more with the fate of Russia in historical rather than geopolitical terms.

The critical response to *Urga* reflects the attitude to Mikhalkov in a changed and changing society. After *Dark Eyes*, which was – with the exception of Tarkovsky – the first Soviet-Russian film co-produced with the West and entered into a major international competition, the first signs of envy appeared among Soviet critics of the time, understandably arguing the better quality of *Mechanical Piano* over the Italian film. *Urga* was nominated for the Oscar award in 1993, and won the Grand Prix at the 48th International Film Festival in Venice in 1991 (against films by Werner Herzog, Isztván Szábo and Peter Greenaway), as well as the Felix of the European Film Academy in 1993. Moreover, it was the first Russian film after Tarkovsky's *Ivan's Childhood* to win the Golden Lion. The competition with Tarkovsky arose again and again in Soviet criticism which pointed out that Tarkovsky never catered for the West, while he also did not live long enough after his emigration to attract the full scale of hatred from his countrymen.[17] Moreover, it would seem that Tarkovsky was less preoccupied with the image of Russia than with the image of time. A film that exposed Soviet people as popular monsters, that treated the Mongols as predecessors, that praised the union with nature and advocated tribal rituals and traditions, that sold wilderness in favour of contemporary Russian life and modern civilisation – such a film was awarded major international awards. This caused an outrage in critical responses to the film, which are excellently summarised in the view of the Russian cultural observer and journalist of Radio Liberty, Peter Vail:

> The director is sophisticated and refined, but he allows himself almost everywhere to lapse into *poshlost* (vulgarity) and didacticism. [...] It is assumed that Mikhalkov carefully presents to the West a suitably wrapped Russian soul. But if the product is in demand for some years, it is not only a question of marketing and advertising but also of quality.[18]

The critic and international festival adviser Andrei Plakhov in his review offers an explanation for the rejection of Mikhalkov's work in his own country: 'In fact, Mikhalkov is valued abroad because of his ability to cultivate the strange and fascinating myth of the Russian soul without being tiresome and with obvious attraction.'[19]

If *Dark Eyes* had damaged Mikhalkov's reputation – the Soviet protégé working abroad and earning international awards – then *Urga* ruined his standing among colleagues and critics. From this point onward, Mikhalkov's films would be classified as commercial kitsch (*kliukva*) for export only. The fact that Mikhalkov's subsequent films were box office hits in Russia rather than abroad goes some way to discredit this common view. With commercial and Western success, Mikhalkov was clearly no longer making 'auteur' cinema, and thus became the enemy of the Soviet intelligentsia, which was itself losing its footing in a period of general commercialisation and consumerism. Criticism was levelled at the film's popular appeal rather than at Mikhalkov's nationalistic views, which began to shift from the visual onto the narrative plane. The scorn for Mikhalkov and his work would develop further in a period when he would himself begin to muddle his public image with the views expressed in his films, and when his Russophilia would obtrude on his work as a film-maker.

> Beginning with Oblomov he [Mikhalkov] confirms: we lost our roots, got bogged down by speed and pragmatism, destroyed the basis of traditional morals. As a result we have not become Europe and betrayed our national culture. [...] Oriental tendencies, conservative Russian themes and exalted pantheism came together, reaching a general peak in the last film [*Urga*].[20]

6. Russia's Past in the Present: 1991–1999

After the collapse of the Soviet Union in 1991 Russia's film industry underwent major shake-ups. The formerly state-run studios were replaced by private studios; the state-managed distribution system collapsed entirely before private investors had time to refurbish cinemas; and the role of the producer had to be re-invented and learnt from scratch after 70 years of state demand and state order.[1] In the years immediately following the collapse of the Soviet Union the number of films produced annually doubled, due to money laundering through the film industry; then film production dropped sharply when these sources became unavailable. In this period of turmoil Mikhalkov founded his own production company, and produced two commercially successful films.

The 1990s were overshadowed by several wars, and major ethnic conflicts were flaring up in the southern regions of the former Soviet empire. These were largely caused by regions with autonomous status within the former Soviet republics claiming full independence after the collapse of the union (Chechnya was an autonomous region within the Russian Federation – a constituent part of the USSR; Abkhazia was an independent region within the Soviet republic of Georgia). In 1992 a war broke out between Georgia and Abkhazia. The first Chechen war (1994–1996) was almost immediately followed by the second Chechen war, involving also Daghestani and Ingush partisans.

In 1993 Yeltsin disbanded the parliament (Duma), transferring more power to rule by decree upon himself, and overthrowing an attempted government coup led by General Rutskoi in October 1993. By 1996 the political situation had stabilised, and Yeltsin was re-elected president. The electoral campaign was strongly manipulated by the mass media – in the hands of oligarchs – while political parties secured their superiority in the elections by investing in shares in the media industry. Financial instability led to an economic crash in August

1998. Yeltsin's rule was shaken by conflicts, by scandals over the president's alcohol consumption and his related ill-health, by economic crises (the deregulation of prices, pyramid schemes, tax evasion, money laundering, media piracy, the devaluation of the rouble, inflation, and finally the crash) and by lawlessness in the mass media. The period was further destabilised by the frequent change of prime ministers – Chernomyrdin, Primakov, Stepanov, Kirienko. On 31 December 1999 Yeltsin resigned, leaving Vladimir Putin as acting president. Putin was confirmed as president in the elections of March 2000. In the 1990s, when the country most needed a strong leadership, its president had been rocked by several scandals; at the same time, Yeltsin had steered the country during the brisk transition from communism to capitalism, which might be expected to be characterised by swings from one extreme to another. Yeltsin became a cartoon figure who was not taken seriously – although he had consolidated power.

Mikhalkov acted only rarely during this period. One of his most significant roles – that of the mayor in a film made by Sergei Gazarov, based on Gogol's *The Government Inspector* [Revizor, 1996] – is an exception. Gazarov wanted to make a popular film and invited a number of star actors, including Evgeni Mironov, Marina Neyolova, Oleg Yankovsky, Armen Dzhigarkhanian and Vladimir Ilyin. In Mikhalkov's interpretation the mayor is sly, cunning and in control of the overall situation that arises after the arrival of the alleged government inspector. He controls the events with a charming authority, oblivious of the fact that he is mistaken about Khlestakov's real identity: he is not the inspector. Mikhalkov makes elaborate use of facial mimicry to emphasise the mayor's readiness to bribe whomever, whenever. Mikhalkov's mayor is convinced that he is doing the right thing; he is full of himself, never thinks of others, but uses them instead as his puppets, who can be deployed or discarded at his will. With his high-pitched voice, his oratorical skills and his talent as a director-controller, Mikhalkov is perfectly cast in this role of a man who never listens but acts only in the way he deems right. Parallels may be drawn not only to the way in which Mikhalkov is perceived in public life but also to Mikhalkov's skills as a political leader.

In the turbulent 1990s Mikhalkov got actively involved in his country's politics. He tried to make political statements, both through his roles and his films, as well as in interviews and other public appearances. At a time when the Soviet state was being disbanded, Mikhalkov took control, as it were, in the role of the mayor. In the films he directed he confronted the issue of Russia's role and its values, which became even more pertinent in the post-Soviet period.[2] Having tended towards a restorative nostalgia in the 1980s with a sense of the Soviet system waning, Mikhalkov now develops further this return to a Soviet past that never existed, and an illusion of Soviet reality rather than its real depiction.

Anna from Six to Eighteen

Still in the transition period, Mikhalkov made a film about his daughter Anna, trying to put his own stamp on the interpretation of the recent history of his country. The film *Anna from Six to Eighteen* is semi-documentary, using documentary footage and scenes filmed privately, and it is dedicated to the memory of Mikhalkov's mother, Natalia Konchalovskaya. Mikhalkov traces the life of his daughter through interviews with her, asking questions about what she likes and what she does not like, what she fears and what she loves, at intervals of approximately one year. These scenes are interspersed with documentary footage relating to the respective periods, with annotations and comments from Mikhalkov's narrative voice.

The film begins at Mikhalkov's summer house on Nikolai's Hill, which belonged to his mother's family. The six-year-old Anna is sitting on a bench, trying to decipher the letters on the cover of a book: Anna Karenina, her namesake. Documentary footage in black and white intercepts the scene: a parade on Red Square, Brezhnev on the mausoleum, Brezhnev's meeting with Honecker, Brezhnev visiting the United States, a black boy arriving in Moscow for the Olympics. All these scenes clearly relate to the year 1980. Mikhalkov's voice-over characterises the Soviet empire as a system that wished to deceive and to be deceived, and as a state that wanted to show unity through identifying an 'enemy', even in sports competition. Anna expresses her fear of the witch Baba Yaga, because she has a long nose and an ugly face; she would like a crocodile; and she does not like beetroot soup (*borshch*). While her answers correspond absolutely to the wishes and fears of a six-year-old, they also reflect the points of reference of a Soviet childhood: the Baba Yaga of the classical fairy tale, the beloved crocodile Gena of Soviet animation,[3] and the dislike of certain kinds of food so common in children.

Mikhalkov explores his ancestry and fills in the background: the change of stress from Mikhálkov to Mikhalkóv to get rid of the aristocratic resonance of their name; the relationship to nineteenth-century painters through his ancestor Vasili Surikov. He also offers an explanation for the making of this film, which is based on an idea that had crossed his mind during the filming of *Oblomov*, when flashbacks showed the child Ilia Oblomov in an empire that had ceased to exist. He thus elevates his own child to a fictional character, a creation of his filmic imagination, and makes her the representative of an entire generation of Soviet children. Documentary footage shows scenes from a Soviet childhood: a new baby is given a name, children in Soviet schools, the Komsomol (Communist Youth League) and its pioneers, the state anthem, and Lenin's reassuring comment on the stability of the Soviet state.

A year later (on 8 August 1981) Anna is running along the path from the house towards her father's car. She likes nature, is afraid of fights, does not like bad people and wants to be intelligent and well behaved. The first signs of disciplining have occurred in the life of the child, and Mikhalkov draws a parallel to his first days at school, when he was turned into a right-hander.

Documentary clips remind us of Brezhnev's speeches and decorations, his funeral (1982) and responses to his death as Anna reads from a textbook about communism. A child is being brought up to be a Soviet citizen. Aged eight, Anna is moved by Brezhnev's death, and hopes that the Soviet people will not forget him. She is afraid of the war (Afghanistan) and loves it when her father is at home; and she likes New Year. Mikhalkov remembers the New Year parties of his childhood. Documentary footage moves onward in time to the funeral of Andropov (1984). Anna is still afraid of war and fighting and wishes for a good leader who will care for the people. She is fond of family life. The ten-year-old is shaken by the rapid change of leadership in her country, where the political leader features as a father figure for the nation. Such children of the nation, young pioneers from all over the Soviet Union, attend the funeral of Chernenko (1985); Gorbachev becomes the new General Secretary. Anna, aged 11, hopes for peace and health. She is saddened by the lack of happiness – the loss of three 'fathers of the nation' in the space of three years has left its trace – but declares that it is not the end of the world. Documentary clips show scenes of the war in Afghanistan as Mikhalkov remembers censored scenes in *Kinfolk* of the soldiers departing for Afghanistan. He summarises the upheavals of the last five years and anticipates a break of two years in filming *Anna* as he leaves for Italy to shoot *Dark Eyes*. During this time Anna's sister Nadia is born.

Black and white frames take us into the period of perestroika with footage of the public appearances of Gorbachev, jazz concerts and discotheques. Anna is fond of her parents, singing, dancing, reading, watching her little sister; she notices certain improvements that perestroika has brought, namely the better quality of textiles. For her a new life has begun, which allows more freedom, and she is impatient to become an adult. The birthday party of the television presenter Sergei Penkin, a former caretaker-singer,[4] with male strippers and transvestites, is a further sign of perestroika, as are the meetings of Gorbachev with world leaders. The Challenger explosion of 1986 and the crash of a Soviet MiG-29 at an air show near Le Bourget in 1989 remind us of the disasters of the late 1980s; the rise of fundamentalism in Iran, the nuclear accident at Chernobyl (1986), and the earthquake in Armenia of 1988 are also remembered.

In December 1988 the family recalls New Year celebrations with Natalia Konchalovskaya, who had died earlier that year. The children, still under the impact of their grandmother's death, fear the deaths of their relatives. Both

Anna and her brother Artem hug their father, just as Iliusha clung to his mother in *Oblomov*.

The footage of events in 1989/90 reminds us of the protests in Tiananmen Square, the dismantling of the Dzerzhinsky statue in Moscow, the fall of the Berlin Wall, the death of Sakharov, a demonstration on Red Square calling for Gorbachev's resignation and the president leaving the tribune on the mausoleum. At 16 Anna no longer fears a war, and would even like to have children. Her trust in the Soviet world is shaken, but the country still inspires feelings of safety and stability. The prayer scene with Iliusha from *Oblomov* is recalled, along with the *Swan Lake* performance screened on television during the attempted coup of 1991. Documentary pictures show Gorbachev's resignation, followed by a change in television culture where foreign influence has taken over.

In September 1991 Anna, now 17, leaves for Switzerland for two years to complete her studies. She fears for her internal world and wants to live in her homeland, the large and beautiful Russia with the woods and fields of her home. She has tears in her eyes when she talks about Russia. Her sister Nadia, then six, is afraid of school and defines her motherland as a small and beautiful place.

The film presents, first and foremost, an interesting picture of the Mikhalkov family. As a document of a child growing up in a country undergoing transformation it has to be viewed with several precautions. Anna is not a typical Soviet child: she stems from a well-known and established artistic family. Moreover, Mikhalkov presents Russia in a favourable light, dwelling on the tradition and heritage of the past, and associates many reactions typical for a teenager with Russia – as, for example, her tears when she leaves, which he attributes to pride in Russia; yet, from a 17-year-old, these are tears for home and family, not for the abstract concept of a country. Mikhalkov's narrative voice interprets and comments; it intrudes rather than allowing the child to speak for herself. Mikhalkov draws parallels to his own childhood and provides a voice-over for the documentary sequences, making sure that his authorial presence is always felt. Finally, Mikhalkov bullies his daughter into saying things to the camera she does not want to say. Anna is rather shy and it is clear that she hates this role but does it to please her father, with the exception of the first shot, when Anna is six years old and – as a six-year-old would – enjoys the novelty of the camera's attention. The film actually offers a rather negative view of the father figure Mikhalkov, lacking tact and comprehension when filming his children, and inflating the status of his own family into the public sphere. By excluding parents and presenting a child in direct relation to political and social events Mikhalkov lays the blame for indoctrination and stifling, discipline and conformity at the feet of school and state. The role of the parents is ignored, with the sole exception of the frame when Mikhalkov hugs the children when they are shocked after the death of their grandmother.

Mikhalkov summarises in the film itself his idea and aim in making the montage film. 'When I began to make the film I wanted to understand where the point lies when these two childhoods depart from each other [...]: they were separated by faith and the absence of God. We have lost the respect for life and death. We turned life into a television serial, death into a computer game.'[5] Mikhalkov's ambition in this film is grand: to show the influence of the state, empire or Soviet, on a child and draw conclusions about the relationship between systems and the eternal values of life and death, eclipsing Western influence (Oblomov's Russia and Brezhnev's Soviet Union). The film is also rather pretentious in elevating his daughter's personal life to the level of national and international history. This ambition behind the project is what made the film one of the most disputed of Mikhalkov's works, and a film that has received hardly any critical attention. The making of a film about the Soviet period and its collapse prepares the ground for the restoration and the correction of Mikhalkov's perspective on life in the 1930s in *Burnt by the Sun*.

Burnt by the Sun

With *Burnt by the Sun* Mikhalkov made another film about his love for Russia, despite the devastation of the Stalinist epoch. On a Sunday in June 1936 the secret service (NKVD) officer Mitia (Oleg Menshikov) accepts and carries out a special assignment: the arrest of the Red Army Commander Kotov (Mikhalkov) at his family's dacha near Moscow. Meanwhile, Kotov enjoys domestic life with his wife Marusia (Ingeborga Dapkunaite) and daughter Nadia (Nadia Mikhalkova). Mitia, a friend of the family and Marusia's first love, arrives and spends the day with the family, taking Kotov with him back to Moscow in the evening. Upon his return to Moscow Mitia succeeds in his second suicide attempt (having tried to shoot himself the day before): he cuts his wrists in the bath.

The film contrasts the pre-Revolutionary lifestyle of the intelligentsia (Marusia's father was a musician, her uncle is a professor of Roman law in the faculty of history) with that of the Soviet reality of Revolutionary leaders (Kotov), juxtaposes the ideals of the Whites against those of the Reds, and ultimately insists on the destructive power of political ideas as opposed to personal happiness. Mikhalkov returned to a pre-Revolutionary, beautiful setting, never condemning Bolshevism and blaming the betrayal of ideas on the Whites; as it were, they annihilated the potential for opposition to Bolshevism.

Russia's Past in the Present: 1991–1999   105

Burnt by the Sun is set at the beginning of the great purges under Stalin and before the show trials, which are, however, looming on the horizon. The film anticipates the Great Terror that would soon become manifest: while it is still possible for a high-ranking officer such as Kotov to believe in the justice of the system, the threat is tangible, audible and visible throughout, but clear to him only by the end of the film. The film captures the last moments before the show trials made such a firm belief as Kotov's in Revolutionary ideals impossible, and conveys a pre-Revolutionary lifestyle that really did survive into the 1930s in exceptional circumstances.[6]

The film's title draws on the 1930s tango 'Utomlennoe solntse' ('The Weary Sun'), changing the grammatical correlation to 'Utomlennye solntsem' – 'those worn out by the sun'. The film is dedicated to those who were burnt by the sun of the Revolution. The title creates an assonance of 'Burnt by the Sun' with another grand narrative of American history, 'Gone with the Wind' (in Russian 'Unesennye vetrom'), attempting to appeal to a wider audience.

The film begins and ends with a view of the red stars on the Moscow Kremlin spires, which were actually only put up in 1937 for the 20th anniversary of the October Revolution. The action departs from and returns to Moscow: NKVD officer Mitia arrives at his Moscow flat and accepts a special assignment. He travels to the country dacha to arrest Kotov and brings him back to Moscow. Mitia's Moscow flat is located in the grey building that was the government apartment block, the 'House on the Embankment',[7] with a close view of the centre of political power (of the Reds), while the 'Whites' – the intellectual Golovin family – live on the periphery, on the outskirts, at least for the summer. *Burnt by the Sun* operates within a closed circular structure in terms of time: the story begins at 6 a.m. and ends at 7 a.m. the following morning. The day portrayed in the film is a long and happy day for a little girl whose ideals remain unshattered throughout,[8] while it is a day that changes the family's life for good.

The circular structure of time and space enhances the closed system of the film's narrative: there is no way out, either in time or space; the characters are entrapped. Outside the capital reigns the vastness of the Russian countryside. Yet here, too, enclosures dominate: the garden of the dacha is surrounded by a fence, and Nadia is forbidden to open the gate. Outside the garden, in the street, potential dangers lurk: the tanks, the black limousine, the evacuation exercise. The enclosure represents simultaneously safety and entrapment.

The interior of the dacha offers a security that cannot be found outside: inside everything is where it belongs, while there are no directions outside. The countryside is unmapped territory: the truck driver is disorientated and gets nowhere with his request for directions; moreover, the letters of the address have been obliterated. In the same way, many people would be 'effaced' during the purges. While the truck is moving in circles in search of the address, Kotov may know the way out. Yet knowledge is dangerous: for Kotov it ends with a bruised face; for the driver with death.

While the truck driver is blundering around the countryside, seeking to find his way on a vertical plane, the balloon (dirigible) is built to go upward into the air: it is designed to conquer space and offer an aerial view (as do the aeroplanes that Kotov hails in the fields as beautiful constructions that do not ruin the fields). The dirigible fits fully into the concept of the conquest of space and territory so common in Stalinist culture.[9]

The film explores the marriage between the old Russian intelligentsia (Marusia) and the Revolutionary system (Kotov). The possibility of such a marriage, or the compatibility of the two systems, is addressed: the marriage is based on lies (Kotov has never confessed his involvement in sending Mitia away), and held together by Marusia's attempt to forget the past. The alliance survives, mainly because of Kotov's energy and (sexual) power. It survives, however, only in a place that eclipses Soviet reality and continues with past traditions. The dacha is an artificial environment, out of space and out of time. Mitia is introduced to the viewer in terms of real time (radio) and real space (Moscow). This reality destroys the illusion of a past life in a house

13. *Burnt by the Sun*, lunch at the dacha: Vsevolod Konstantinovich (Viacheslav Tikhonov), Mitia (Oleg Menshikov), the aunts and Marusia (Ingeborga Dapkunaite); Nadia and Kotov with their backs to the camera

protected from the outside world by gates and fences. Again, Mikhalkov plays with the permanence of time in a space symbolising the past.

Three generations link the pre-Revolutionary past to the present: the fathers, whose lifestyle from the past is dying out (Vsevolod Konstantinovich); the children of the present times (Kotov, Mitia, Marusia); and the future generation, represented by Nadia. The absence and presence of parents is important: Mitia's parents died during the Civil War and he was adopted by Marusia's father, cared for by his tutor Philippe. Stalin is a father figure to Mitia: when Stalin appears as an all-powerful pagan god, rising (on the banner attached to the balloon) as the sun is setting,[10] it becomes clear that he is a father surrogate to Mitia, who has no other family ties. Nadia's belief in the system and in the Soviet ideal is never shattered: she greets the pioneers in a professional, military manner. Kotov strengthens her enthusiasm, telling her about Soviet power, which builds such flat roads that her heels will remain soft and rosy; she is not afraid of the men in the car, even sitting at the wheel when they leave with Kotov, returning to the dacha humming the title song.

In the atmosphere of the dacha Marusia's family reminisce about pre-Revolutionary times, a life enriched by traditions and values, by culture (music, dance, plays), which returns to the dacha with Mitia and from which Kotov is excluded: he has no education. Mitia belongs culturally and socially with Marusia's family, but he has been alienated from it by Kotov, who recruited him for the secret service. Now he brings pre-Revolutionary activities back and excludes Kotov, who cannot speak French or dance the cancan. The political past forms the subject of a brief conversation during the football match, when Kotov reminds Mitia of the facts as he remembers them: Mitia was an officer for the Whites before becoming a secret agent for the OGPU in 1923 so that he could return from emigration. Mitia obediently rewrites Kotov's past according to the instructions of the NKVD: Kotov had been a German spy since 1920 and worked for the Japanese since 1923. The past is, on the one hand, a happy memory; on the other, it is a part of history to be rewritten according to the dominant perspective on the political past at any given time.

Mitia believed in the system when he trusted the secret service in their promise to repatriate him and then let him off the hook. A naïve belief, perhaps, but such naïvety was common among Russian émigré circles in Europe in the 1920s. Kotov, meanwhile, took everything Mitia had longed for and betrayed him. Kotov claims that his actions were always motivated by a sense of duty for his country, whereas Mitia acted out of fear. Yet Mitia has acted in defence of that pre-Revolutionary world in which Kotov now lives, like a parasite, with a beautiful and intelligent wife and a lovely child.

Mitia's decisions are made for personal reasons, whereas Kotov is a military man whose personal life comes second to duty. The axis of the plot, however, is not the issue of Mitia wishing to destroy the world to which he no longer belongs; instead, he aims to annihilate Kotov's attempt to live with the best of two worlds simultaneously. Mitia is politically successful, but his personal life has failed. Kotov has personal happiness and political power, and he loses both. Mitia realises the potential permanence of personal happiness as opposed to the transience of political success: he has finished with his life already at the beginning of the film and leaves it to chance (Russian roulette) whether he fulfils this assignment or not; if he does not arrest Kotov, then somebody else will. The system is indestructible. Kotov enjoys 'paternal' protection from Stalin but, when he realises that a change has taken place and Stalin is now a father figure for Mitia, he cries like a child disappointed by his parent and deprived of paternal love.

The film raises the question of where the borderline lies between victim and oppressor, between the victim Kotov and the victim Mitia. Although one might argue at first sight that there is a crude dividing line between the positive hero Kotov and the offender and destroyer Mitia, between Kotov's Soviet heroism and Mitia's Western decadence, the film is much more complex than that. Kotov is a mere executor of Stalin's political will, and acts under the illusion of having control (believing to the end that he can still rely on Stalin's support); Mitia, by contrast, has tried to preserve his integrity: he acts, aware of the fact that he is a mere arm of power, an executor, an actor. The comparison to Platonov lies nearby, who is as passive and lazy as the other characters in *Mechanical Piano*, but aware of his passivity.

The choice of the popular actor Oleg Menshikov for the part of Mitia is instrumental in bringing out the positive features in the NKVD officer. Mitia appears as an old, blind man emerging from the Young Pioneers marching past the dacha: he is a blank page onto which any history and any identity can be written. In order to win Nadia's heart he poses as Father Frost (the Russian equivalent of Santa Claus) and as a magician; in order to gain entrance into the house he claims to be a doctor. He pretends to be married with three children, yet he is a sad, lonely man. He can adopt any role; indeed, he needs to do so in order to give his life a meaning, at least temporarily. He recites the tunes he taught Marusia, repeats the steps he learnt in Paris, quotes Hamlet, plays an invalid at the beach to be helped up by a fat lady, and 'performs' a dive into the river. His every movement is a calculated action, a performance. There is no other way for him to return to the past than by creating a carnival atmosphere that allows him to behave like a child and play all sorts of – forbidden – games. He needs to create masks for himself, rather than a personality; he lacks psychological depth and, burdened with his role, he cannot change or reveal his emotions.[11]

If Mitia is an actor who performs roles, Kotov is an image that cannot change. Mitia wrote this part for himself, whereas Kotov is a portrait in a world replacing its idols. Effigies of the Leader were displayed everywhere in the 1930s; Stalin's portrait features in central episodes in the film and finally rises on the balloon's banner. Kotov's portraits are also displayed everywhere, and the encounter with him has a similar effect on people to the 'unforgettable encounters' with Stalin portrayed in Soviet films of the 1930s and 1940s: recognition of the goal of socialism. Indeed, Kotov somewhat resembles Stalin, with his huge moustache. Yet images may collapse, and Kotov is only an image. The popularity of effigies of any other leader but Stalin can be compared to the rivalry between Kirov and Stalin in 1934 before Stalin instructed the NKVD to eliminate his rival. Mitia's reaction to the portrait of the Great Leader rising on the balloon underlines his acceptance of his role as an executor. Mitia is about to light a cigarette stuck between his lips when his face contracts into a huge grin: he has done the job, as the leader wanted; he has played his role.

When Mitia first appears, he emerges from a group of marching pioneers who are singing the 'Aviators' March' (1920). The song anticipates the 1930s' call for a varnished and perfected reality, while it also echoes two themes relevant to the film: the birds that fly too high get burnt by fireballs; and the theme of aeroplanes that conquer territory. 'We are born to make a fairy tale come true', a line from the song, is the premise upon which Mitia enters the house. Mitia speaks the truth through fairy tales: he is from the West (the Maghreb) and he recalls the happy past in the form of a fairy tale. In a tale with inverted names, Mitia tells the story of the boy Yatim, who had to fight in the war, and when he returned the girl Yasum had become a beautiful princess, with whom he fell in love. Then an important man took Yasum away from him and sent him abroad. Nadia understands the principle of fairy tales very well: she expects a happy ending, and when Yatim and Yasum do not marry she correctly assumes that the 'important man' must be an ogre. She also understands the principle of the inversion of names and applies it to herself: she figures out that she would be Yadan in the story. Nadia transposes herself into fairy worlds, but does not transpose the fairy tale world into reality. The principle advocated in the Soviet march does not work: we do not turn the fairy tale into reality, but instead make reality a fairy story, a myth.

The main line of the character relationships is built on the duality that lies in the confrontation between Mitia and Kotov, rivals for Marusia's affection. Mitia returns to the house of the woman he loves, yet he peppers the conversation with constant reminders of her not as a young girl but as a child. Mitia is clearly indicating that he is not there to claim Marusia back. He acts in a way to protect Marusia, who is understandably shaken up in her artificially built and carefully created emotional security when he arrives. Mitia is very playful with Nadia and relates extremely well to her, despite the fact that he has no children. Yet he recognises in the six-year-old Nadia the girl Marusia whom he took to the Bolshoi Theatre and whom he taught the piano. His relation to the little girl Marusia explains not only his experience of handling children but also why he is so fond of Nadia. In fact, he receives from Nadia the attention he got from the little Marusia, the attention he no longer elicits from the woman who is now Kotov's wife. Nadia is a substitute for Marusia.

While Kotov combines the world of the present with that of the past, the harmony of Marusia's family life with his military career, Mitia never succeeds in getting a share of both. Yet this is what he longs for all the time: to side with the Whites and to stay in Russia; to return to Russia with the help of the secret service and then quit. His wish to have the best of both worlds means compromise, and this is what he cannot reach. His dilemma is reflected in an everyday banality: in his reply to Nadia's question whether he wants 'tea with jam' or 'coffee with milk', Mitia says he would like 'coffee with jam'. As a result, he gets neither.

Colour symbolism dominates costumes and clothing: the *dachniki* are all in white, seated on their rattan furniture. A hint of blue sometimes complements the white of the costumes (stripes on a shirt, a blue edge on a collar, a blue blouse), reflecting the colour range of the Russian flag. Their white dress (a reference also to the 'White' army) is contrasted to the grey of the NKVD officers' suits and of the concrete structure of the House on the Embankment, symbolising power. The balloon that pulls up Stalin's portrait is of a silvery grey. The colour black features only on the car that comes to take Kotov and Mitia back to Moscow. The colour red is associated with the Soviet way of life: the Young Pioneers' ties, the flags on the trumpets, the flags at the beach and in the street, the banners on the House on the Embankment and on the construction site of the balloon, the stars on the Kremlin towers, but – most importantly – the banner with the portrait of Stalin that rises on the horizon at the end of the film. Red is also the colour of the blood on Kotov's face and in Mitia's bath. It is implied here that the Soviet power represented by the colour red is the same as blood, and built on the blood of the people.

Twice in the film the special effect of a fireball is used. First, when Mitia tells the fairy tale about the past, the fireball emerges on the river, whizzes through the house and settles over the wood, where it eventually collides with a falcon and crashes into a single tree, which burns down. The destruction of a bird and a single tree accompanies the point in the narrative when Mitia loses Marusia for the first time. The second fireball effect accompanies Mitia's physical destruction, his suicide. The fireball is red and can also be understood as a symbol for the Soviet system in an extension of the colour symbolism discussed above. In this reading the system destroys people in an indiscriminate manner. The effect is symbolic and not integrated in the overall realism of the film.[12] It obtrudes as artificial, although it is reported in the newspaper article that Philippe reads at the beginning of the film, and it is unreal in that nobody notices the fireball.

Kotov and Mitia both faced choices between life and death at different moments in their past. Mitia claims that he had no choice, and that a choice between life and death is no choice. He left the country without telling Marusia that he was acting on NKVD orders to protect her family, but – and here he is honest – also because he also wanted to live. Kotov says there is always a choice, a choice between life and death. Like Mitia, Kotov does not want anyone to know that he will be arrested in order not to upset the peace in the house. Ironically, he has no choice any more.

Kotov has something to live for in the ideal and perfect construction of the future. Mitia has no sense in his life. Kotov's life is taken: Mitia takes his own. He puts an end to being used for further tasks (the phone keeps ringing, possibly with more special assignments, while he lies in the bath). He knows that he is an arm of the system, and he – who claimed that there was no choice – makes a choice: to put an end to his life. Kotov makes no choice in the present: he has chosen, once and for all, to trust Stalin; now he makes

14. *Burnt by the Sun*, Kotov (Nikita Mikhalkov) and Nadia (Nadia Mikhalkova) in the boat

the choices. Mitia is only an executive: if he does not carry out the arrest, somebody else will. Mitia is a loser: he is doomed to defeat; he has lost the war, love, life. The absence of love alluded to in the title song defines the theme of the film and is the reason for Mitia's behaviour.

Burnt by the Sun dwells on the beauty of Russia, on the lifestyle of the past, which is not, in the film, destroyed by the Bolshevik Kotov. Continuing the glorification of Bolshevism begun in *At Home Among Strangers* and *Slave of Love*, Mikhalkov here, too, lays no blame for the destruction at Kotov's feet. 'Yes, Bolshevism has not brought happiness to our country. But is it morally correct on the basis of this indisputable fact to put under doubt the life of entire generations only on the grounds that people happened to be born not in the best of times?'[13]

Mitia is a mere arm of the system, and Stalin's totalitarian regime is thus interpreted as an inevitable part of history that neither Kotov nor Mitia are directly responsible for. The film relieves the individual of responsibility for history, and glorifies not only the Russia of the past but also Bolshevism (albeit defeated in the 1930s). Mikhalkov thus creates an apologia for what the Soviet system turned great Russia into and sways between a neo-Leninist and Russophile position.[14]

Mikhalkov presents Soviet reality as more illusory than the fairy tale, inverting the relationship between fact and fiction. The fairy tale contains a confession, which is a myth, while the present is the illusion of life. Thus, neither past nor present is authentic. Mikhalkov longs for a past when it was possible to believe in ideals, when there were ideals. These are absent in the present; they are about to disappear this day in June 1936. Mikhalkov thus infers the need for a Utopia from past to present; once ideals are destroyed, people die at the hands of the system, or at their own hands. Mikhalkov here makes a worrying comment on the present of Russian society, which – in 1994 – clearly lacked any such ideals. By casting himself as a kind Bolshevik commander, who believes in the ideals of the Revolution and, furthermore, is a perfect father to his child, he offers himself in the role of a leader of the people, but one who would return to the roots of socialism, or – in fictional terms – to the spirit of *At Home Among Strangers*. This confusion of fiction and reality leads to the portrayal of a political Utopia, which Mikhalkov would gradually mistake for an authentic ideal. It is from this angle that Tatiana Moskvina's comment stems: 'Any person who proposes himself and his life as a universally valid lyrical Utopia is in danger of losing the understanding of his rational contemporaries.'[15]

The period between inception and realisation for *Burnt by the Sun* was extremely short. Mikhalkov discussed the idea for the film in the summer of 1993 with his co-author Rustam Ibragimbekov, and they began to write the script immediately in a dacha in Nizhny Novgorod. Mikhalkov gained the support of the governor of Nizhny Novgorod, Boris Nemtsov, and decided to begin shooting immediately, although the film had, as of then, no budget. Mikhalkov has explained this by not wanting to let another year elapse during which his daughter Nadia would have outgrown the phase when he saw her best fit to play her part in the film.

Mikhalkov and TriTe managed the Russian distribution of the film themselves, rather than contracting a distributor. They had to claim a high rental charge from cinemas to recoup production costs, and therefore they encouraged regional administrations to find sponsors, so that cinemas could pay the rental charge for the film without raising ticket prices. Another condition of the lease was that no illegal video copies would be made, so as to avoid financial loss through the sale of pirated copies.[16]

Burnt by the Sun was premiered in the competition programme of the International Film Festival in Cannes in May 1994, where it was awarded the Grand Prix of the Jury, the second most important award after the Palme d'Or, which went to Quentin Tarantino's *Pulp Fiction*. Moreover, *Burnt by the Sun* won the Grand Prix jointly with the Chinese film *Living* [Huozhe, 1994] by Bin Wang and Xleochun Zhang. Mikhalkov was appalled at getting only the second prize, and at having to share it, when his ambition had been to be the first Russian since Mikhail Kalatozov in 1958[17] to take the Palme. However, winning the Oscar a year later was no bad achievement either. The first scandal had begun: the Russian press reported the failure of the film to win the main award and, instead of praising how well a Russian film had done – at long last – at an international festival, they shouted 'defeat'. Further rumours followed that Mikhalkov would never participate in the Cannes Film Festival again; such rumours were proved false by the European premiere of *The Barber of Siberia* at the Cannes Festival in 1999.

The reviews in the Russian press in late 1994 and 1995 were largely neutral, praising a film that had by then received major international acclaim and fared better than any other Russian film abroad. Most critics elaborated on the Chekhovian theme, regarding *Burnt by the Sun* as a continuation of *An Unfinished Piece for a Mechanical Piano* in transposing the Chekhovian characters of the earlier film into the 1930s, and many critics debated the issue of the filmmaker's condemnation or non-condemnation of Revolutionary force and the inertia of the intelligentsia.

Negative comments can be found among the formerly dissident intelligentsia, who still believe that art is designed to be understood only by the selected few, but not by wider audiences, not to mention the 'masses'. Only a film that *cannot* be understood by the Western viewer is a good Russian film. If that is the rule, then *Burnt by the Sun* is a *bad* Russian film, since the film – on the whole – can be understood by any viewer. Yet I would contend that a film is like a Russian stacking doll: it offers a multiplicity of layers for interpretation, and the more patient viewer knows of the culture the more layers he/she will discover.

The pivotal issue addressed in this film, as in other films about the Stalin era, is the question of responsibility. In a system such as the Soviet one, where the individual was 'freed' from choice, did the individual have any scope for making decisions? In a totalitarian state, does the individual have any choice, and, if so, where does the choice lie (in Mitia's case, die or collaborate)? Ultimately, who is responsible: the system or the individual? Critics have commented a great deal on the issue of choice and guilt in *Burnt by the Sun*, seeking to ascertain whom the film-maker condemns – the Reds or the Whites; the Revolutionaries or the intelligentsia; dreamers or thinkers.[18]

Overall, the response from Russian critics is typical of their attitude to Nikita Mikhalkov: the film has enjoyed great success with audiences both at home and abroad, because it is not made for an elite audience, and therefore it is despised by the Russian intelligentsia. The same pattern is true for the critical response to *The Barber of Siberia*.

The Barber of Siberia

The Barber of Siberia represents Mikhalkov's attempt to make a blockbuster and to offer moral guidance to an audience at a time when the mainstream of Russian film-makers portrayed the bleakness, the abyss and the degeneration surrounding them. *The Barber of Siberia* shapes the values of the future by telling a story about Russia's past that elevates the traditions of the East above those of the West, tells a fairy tale without a happy ending and stands in both form and content aloof from Hollywood expectations. The film uses a historical setting for this romantic plot with a positive hero to transport the moral values of the past into the present. In terms of box office it was one of the most successful films in Russia in the 1990s, while its distribution in the West did not bring the desired success.

The Barber of Siberia was written in 1987/88, published in 1992/93 and filmed between 1995 and 1997. The evolution of the script spans the period of reform under Gorbachev, the collapse of the Soviet Union and the emergence of the new Russia. The film was premiered in lavish style in the Kremlin Palace of Congresses on 20 February 1999, the first film to be premiered there in over 20 years, with an extensive publicity campaign (discussed in chapter 1). Tatiana Moskvina has described the film as a sequel to *Dark Eyes*, with its continuation of a view of Russia through the eyes of a foreigner.[19]

The Barber of Siberia tells the story of Jane Callaghan (Julia Ormond), an American woman who travels to Russia in 1885 in order to help the Irish-American inventor Douglas McCracken (Richard Harris) to secure funding for his machine, the 'barber', which is designed to cut down the Siberian forests. McCracken, under pressure from his creditors, has hired Jane to charm General Radlov (Alexei Petrenko), the head of the Military Academy, in order to gain through him the support of Grand Duke Alexei. Jane achieves this task by pretending to be McCracken's daughter and flirting with the self-conscious and vain general, who proposes to her. In her business-orientated approach to life Jane has offered her ability to charm for hire ever since she was abused as a child by her stepfather and forced to fend for herself. Then she meets the cadet Andrei Tolstoy (Oleg Menshikov), who falls in love with her. The cadet Tolstoy has very high moral values: he defends his feelings for Jane in a duel, he humiliates himself when he proposes to Jane in front of the general, and he is prepared to abandon his career for Jane. She, however, continues her intrigues in order to fulfil her contract and get McCracken's papers signed by the Grand Duke. Unwilling to sacrifice her scheme for the sake of love, she spends a day with the general at a Shrovetide fair and encourages him to drink, seeking to compromise him. When Tolstoy sees Jane flirt with the general in the theatre just after she has spent the night with the cadet, he attacks his rival with a violin bow during a performance of *The Marriage of Figaro*, in which Tolstoy plays Figaro. The production by the Military Academy takes place in the presence of the Grand Duke, and Radlov swiftly accuses Tolstoy of an attempt upon the Grand Duke's life. Thus Radlov secures promotion for himself by 'preventing a terrorist act', while Tolstoy is found guilty and sent to a prison camp in Siberia, without ever attempting to defend his actions.

Ten years later Jane has married McCracken, so that her son (Tolstoy's child) will have a father. On the occasion of the launch of McCracken's invention Jane travels to Siberia. As the machine begins the massive destruction of the Siberian taiga, Jane finds the house where Tolstoy now lives with his wife Dunia (formerly a maid in the Tolstoys' Moscow house) and their children. Jane leaves Russia.

The love story of Jane and Andrei Tolstoy is embedded in an English narration by Jane, who, in 1905, writes a letter to her son Andrew (the English version of his father's name, Andrei), a recruit at a US military base. Time and again we see her writing the letter, while her voice reads parts of it, and we see Andrew at the US base, as stubborn as his father and upholding values and principles that he defends with his life: he stands up for Mozart by refusing to repeat a phrase denigrating the composer. Rather than obeying Commander O'Leary's order to denounce Mozart's talent he wears a gas mask for over 24 hours. Andrew's endurance wins out, and the explanation for his stubbornness comes from Jane, who shows the commander a portrait of Andrew's father, the former Russian cadet Tolstoy.

The Barber explores the qualities of the Russian character and juxtaposes them to the traits of Western characters. The way Tolstoy behaves towards Jane parallels the stubborn insistence upon principle displayed by the recruit Andrew – both Russian qualities. The Jane who reflects on the past does so with hindsight, but she is still unable fully to understand Russia, implying that Russia cannot be grasped by reason alone. Jane and McCracken represent a world that is largely deprived of any spiritual ideals, while the Russian cadets are endowed with a sense of honour and love for the fatherland. The Western characters acknowledge only success in business or the achievement of goals, while most of the Russian characters surrender to a fatalistic vision of their life, accepting suffering and solitude.

Jane represents, in the worst sense, family relations in the West. She comes from a broken family: her father has died, her mother remarried; she was abused by her stepfather, who then left her mother. She was never loved, has nothing to believe in or to live for. She has given herself up to selling her services. When she spends the night with Tolstoy she realises his devotion to

15. *The Barber of Siberia*, Tolstoy (Oleg Menshikov) and Jane (Julia Ormond) in the train

her; yet she continues to play her game in order to fulfil her contract for her own financial benefit. Jane gambles, thinking she can both fulfil her contract and achieve happiness with Tolstoy, but the stakes are too high. Love and material benefit are incompatible. She never really understands Tolstoy's pride and honour, taking him instead for an immature boy. Their relationship is not one of love: the love scene happens off-screen and remains unconvincing due to the inability of both Ormond and Menshikov to act 'love'. Tolstoy's family is broken, too, but he manages to uphold moral standards and finds a family substitute in the army. Both Andrei's and Andrew's military superiors are bachelors. Love fails on a human level across all classes of society: even the Tsar, as he himself quips, would have had no children if things had gone the way his wife, the Empress Maria Fedorovna (Princess Dagmar of Denmark), had wished. The only love acceptable for a military man is love for the Tsar and, when Tolstoy places Jane above the Tsar, he betrays the 'Father' of the nation.

Both Captain Mokin and Commander O'Leary are strict, but ready to listen to their cadets and act like father figures. Both are, ultimately, not just concerned with discipline but ready to admit when they have been wrong – and ready to defend 'their' soldiers. Thus life in the military, with its discipline, is endowed with human concern, and the military is idealised. In the absence of intact family life and father figures the military community replaces the family while the Tsar substitutes the father, who is also represented on a lower level by the military commanders. In Mikhalkov's vision the whole of Russian society is transformed into one large family with a patriarch at its head. And Tsar Alexander III is played by Mikhalkov himself.

The film is set in the Russia of Tsar Alexander III (1881–1894), a reactionary and nationalist ruler, who is portrayed as a benevolent tsar, displaying humane traits in his love for children, taking his son Mikhail on horseback to a parade. As the cadets stand to attention, the camera captures a sparrow at the cadets' feet and closes up on the small creature, a shot that conveys how the Tsar never neglects the small at the expense of the grand. The Tsar is thus presented as an ideal father, for his child as well as for the nation. Such a portrayal is important in the light of the absence of a father figure in so many contemporary Russian films of the post-Soviet period, when soldiers no longer know what they are fighting and dying for – as, for example, in Sergei Bodrov's *The Prisoner of the Mountains* [Kavkazskii plennik, 1996].

Historically, however, the film is inaccurate. In remembering the past Mikhalkov conflates time, portraying a Russia that is drawn more from artistic representation than reality. Many film critics have commented over the years on the important role of the director of photography, Pavel Lebeshev, in the creation of Mikhalkov's films. Lebeshev is capable of creating a painterly view of scenes, such as the Shrovetide in *The Barber*, the views of the valley in

Oblomov, the mansion overlooking the river in *Mechanical Piano*. Mikhalkov is interested more in representation than reality, in mystification rather than fact. He sets his film in the Russia of 1885, when Alexander III was in power, yet his Russia resembles that of the mid-nineteenth century under Alexander II or even Nicholas I. Indeed, the terrorist activities of the Popular Will (*Narodnaia volia*) had come to an end in 1883; there were no fireworks, silver samovars and silk garments during the plebeian festivities of the Shrovetide; French and German, but not English, were spoken in Russia in the nineteenth century; the ritual of the cadets becoming officers was conducted after a fortnight of hard training, and cadets appeared before the Tsar sweaty and exhausted, not groomed and fresh; and there were no travel restrictions in 1885 for foreigners visiting Siberia. The direct line to the Grand Duke in Radlov's office, on the other hand, is a gadget of a later, distinctly Soviet period.[20] Mikhalkov chooses to glorify aspects of nineteenth-century life that never co-existed.[21]

The moral values of the young Russian cadet Tolstoy are held up as a model, designed to help contemporary audiences value and love their fatherland. The film contains a dichotomy between the traditions of the East and the West. Russian traditions are portrayed in great detail, such as 'Forgiveness Sunday' and the Shrovetide celebrations in the week before Lent. The spectator is presented with this image of Russia through the eyes of a foreign visitor or tourist, Jane, who is capable only of imitating Russian habits without ever comprehending the concepts behind them. Indeed, she speaks no Russian. Taken together with the demonisation of Western influence this would seem to be one obstacle in making the film successful in the West, especially since this foreigner is a compulsive liar: Jane has played so many roles in her life that she just sheds one role and becomes a new person. Her roles and her history change so rapidly that one is never quite sure what to believe, and she appears to adapt her story to each changing situation very swiftly. She pretends, for example, to be McCracken's daughter, but then admits she is not. On another occasion she tells McCracken that her husband drowned in the Nile, while she tells Radlov that he died in battle. In reality, Jane was never married before coming to Russia.

In breaking with her character Jane does nothing of substance to save Tolstoy. She is not inventive and cannot even think of a role when asked what relation she has to Tolstoy at the prison gate. Dunia, on the other hand, is ready to strike Jane with a sickle when she comes into their house in Siberia and poses a threat to their family. Conversely, McCracken has an ideal he believes in, to the extent that it dominates his life and he forgets everything else, taking no interest in the world around him, and he is prepared to die for his ideal when he tries to hang himself when funding is uncertain. The machine that embodies the meaning of his life conquers nature and makes him its master in a knight's uniform, confronting the first attack of the machine. Mikhalkov raises the environmentalist issue of the destruction of nature.

The values upheld in the film are typical of the nineteenth century, which Mikhalkov connects to the beauty and the deep sense of Russian folk traditions. Likewise, the heroism displayed by Tolstoy is possible only in a setting of the nineteenth century. *The Barber of Siberia* instils nostalgia in the spectator, not for the Soviet past but for Tsarist, pre-Revolutionary Russia, related to the present through the historical event that dominated 1998: the laying to rest of the remains of the last Tsar and his family, the Romanovs, in St Petersburg in July 1998.

The Barber of Siberia offers a moral statement by asserting the need to have principles; it presents a positive hero with the potential to instil hope in contemporary Russian audiences. The film is designed to boost the image of Russia as a nation with high ideals, unwilling to compromise, and with a strong leadership. The film is past and future, objective and subjective, national and international all at once, attempting to create a myth for audiences at home and abroad. This is, ultimately, the function of the American dream-factory as described by Mikhalkov himself at the fourth congress of the FU in May 1998: '[People] know the America that the cinema has shown them. America has forced the world to perceive it through cinema.'[22] *The Barber of Siberia* strives for just that: to offer an idealised view of Russia to foreign audiences through the eyes of a foreigner. It would seem that Mikhalkov had

16. *The Barber of Siberia*, McCracken (Richard Harris) and his invention

misunderstood something about the role of American cinema outside Russia: he made a non-commercial feature film on the budget of a Hollywood movie that failed to reach an international market.

The responses to the film were diverse. Most film critics and former members of the intelligentsia, as well as student audiences, tended to dislike the film, while the crowds adored it. The longing for a Russia lost, the theme of patriotism for a country that had – in 1999 – no ideals to proffer, dominated comments on the film. 'The film is great [...] it will take the Oscar,' commented a young woman, although the film had at that point already been rejected by the Academy for not fulfilling the requirement of theatrical release before 31 October 1998.[23] 'This is a film of a patriot. We are patriots too,' said an old woman. 'I regret that we have lost all of that,' commented the mother of a 13-year-old. 'It shows the reality of the Russian people, Russian characters. We are like those people in the film, at least that's what we would like to think,' a young couple opined, acknowledging at least the possibility that they might be looking at a myth rather than an authentic picture of their past.[24] 'I liked the film a lot. I watched a lot of good films and somehow never considered myself a patriot. I am ashamed to talk about that, but I don't think I love my country. But I felt how it needs to be loved – with the eyes of Mikhalkov,' commented a young girl.[25]

What made the film more popular than *Dark Eyes*? First, the possibility of reaching a mass audience in the Russian film market of the late 1990s, when people were pining for a Russian-made blockbuster, and cinemas could attract large numbers of viewers. Second, the context: while, in 1986 Russian audiences were overwhelmed with films about the past, films that had been censored and films that were addressing previously forbidden themes such as alcoholism, drugs and crime, in the late 1990s they were waiting for a film that glorified their country. Thus, although the two films share a longing for a non-authentic past and a non-authentic Russia, Mikhalkov's restorative nostalgia with its nationalist and patriotic overtones worked in Italy in 1986 but not in Russia, while *The Barber* triumphed in Russia but not in the West, which had seen another side of Russia – one dominated by chaos, instability and unpredictability in the 1990s.

As a political manifesto the film contains a strangely nationalistic statement for the future of Russia, envisaging the resurrection of order and discipline that would reinstate a value system and thus benefit the Russian population. In this sense he pre-empted the stability brought about by Putin's rule after the chaos of the Yeltsin era.

A theme that accompanies all Mikhalkov's films is the beauty of the Russian countryside, which harbours the love for the motherland (*rodina*, the country where one is born – derived from the word *rodit'*, to give birth) with its high moral values and the readiness for sacrifice. The threat of destruction through progress always comes from the West – the creation of a factory for the making of unbreakable glass (*Dark Eyes*), the bicycle (*Oblomov*), the machine for chopping down the woods (*Barber*), the factory in the steppe (*Urga*). Russia's fate is the preservation of man's unity with nature, and the conservation of unspoilt nature. Mikhalkov's films of the 1990s tend to move towards a sense of patriotism, replacing the concept of the 'motherland' with the 'fatherland' (*otechestvo* [*otets* means father], a concept that is associated in Russian with – military – service for the country). The longing not for 'Mother Russia' but for a fatherland emerges strongly in Mikhalkov's post-Soviet films: in *Anna* it is manifest in the film-maker's obsession with himself as a father; in *Burnt by the Sun* there is the concern with the father figure, its absence, and the illusion of Stalin as a surrogate father; and in *Barber* Mikhalkov casts himself as a father of the family and the nation. Mikhalkov thus replaces the concept of Mother Russia with a more masculine model of his homeland. The films of the 1990s express a Russian nationalist view in attributing destruction and negative influence to characters from the West or who have been exposed to the West: Mitia in *Burnt by the Sun* and Jane in *The Barber*. At the same time, though, Mikhalkov co-produced his films with a French producer, and heavily relied on the model of the American film industry in his vision for Russian cinema. Ideals may be one thing, the practicalities of everyday life are another.

Concluding Remarks

The 'Family'

When looking at Mikhalkov's films the most striking thing is not the use of cinematic devices, an extravagant set, stunning costumes or the performance of an actor, but the ensemble work. Mikhalkov has worked for much of his career with the same designer and scriptwriter, the same cameraman, the same composer: Alexander Adabashian, Pavel Lebeshev and Eduard Artemiev.

In the 1970s and 1980s Mikhalkov worked with Adabashian,[1] who wrote filmscripts and screen adaptations with Mikhalkov and served, together with Alexander Samulekin, as designer. For the films of the 1990s, *The Barber of Siberia* and *Burnt by the Sun*, Mikhalkov parted from Adabashian and collaborated on his scripts with Rustam Ibragimbekov. He also chose a new set designer, Vladimir Aronin.[2] While paying attention to detail and period, Aronin endows dress and habitat with a subtle symbolism: the colour symbolism in *Burnt by the Sun*, as well as the historical accuracy in *The Barber*, testify to his concern with detail.

The cameraman Pavel Lebeshev[3] has been a long-time collaborator with Mikhalkov, and has worked on all Mikhalkov's films except *Burnt by the Sun* and *Urga* (which were filmed by Vilen Kaliuta) and the Italian co-productions, where an Italian cameraman was employed. In *At Home Among Strangers* he used a hand-held camera for some scenes. The film included some monochrome images, tinted with colour to accentuate their importance. Lebeshev also worked with chiaroscuro (the contrast of light and dark), brightness and shades to express the peripetias of the detective genre.

> Lebeshev offered an essentially different approach. First, the light tends even more to be monochrome [...], while it is organised in blocks of sepia or shaded blue.

There are bursts of red – the flags and banners of the Revolution. The colour reminds us of the paintings of Petrov-Vodkin, of the post-Revolutionary Malevich.[4]

Lebeshev's undoubted talent also lay in the creation of a painterly style in each frame, arranging scenes in a way reminiscent of nineteenth-century painting, which assisted the creation of an artistic rather than realistic portrayal of the nineteenth century and a precise 'retro' atmosphere for the Soviet settings. In *Slave of Love* he exposed the film stock to light before using it, thus increasing the sensitivity of Soviet film stock (*svema*) to light and creating effects normally achievable only on Kodak film, which was not that easily available in the former Soviet Union. In *Oblomov* his preoccupation with valleys, woods and river would reach a climax, both in the scenes with Oblomov at the dacha and with the boy Iliusha on the estate. The green meadows were contrasted with the glittering snow, and both embellished the Russian landscape. Lebeshev was a master in his field, and his camera movements have helped greatly to create the image of 'Mother Russia' associated with Mikhalkov's films.

> In the finale, the meadow is gently green, huge, stretched out, enlarged in size. The figure of the boy, who is lost in the field, seems tiny. The child runs on to the hill and disappears behind it. The camera does not allow the child to disappear – it moves up the hill and pans the vast valley behind the hill. The space in this frame is dynamic. The space moves away from our view with resilient steps, and with each jump it acquires more grandeur. The valley itself is now joyful and bright, like a smile.[5]

Mikhalkov's most permanent companion is the composer Eduard Artemiev,[6] who selected classical music, Russian folk music and Western music to complement or counterpoint key themes, while composing original music for central themes that would recur in the film to underline similarities between situations, both within a film and across films (e.g. the use of 'Adieu' in *Slave of Love* and *Burnt by the Sun*). Mikhalkov often selected tunes himself, which Artemiev then integrated into the film music.

Mikhalkov is a very popular director among the acting community, which is reflected in the brilliant acting performances in his films. Mikhalkov instils trust in his actors and inspires in them a sense that he shares with them the secret of their role.[7] Mikhalkov has 'discovered' and opened new facets in a number of actors over the last 30 years, without ever casting an actor stereotypically in the same type. He has behaved towards his actors like a father: he has protected them from public criticism, blaming camerawork or technical failure if a scene did not come out the way he wanted it. In this 'conspiracy of silence' with his team and the protection of the actor lies the recipe for his successful work with his actors. At the same time Mikhalkov has created, off-screen as much as on-screen, a mythical family unit, in which he was to play the role of a father beyond his time on the set. He has created an illusory world, in which he has continued to play-act.

History Reviewed

Mikhalkov has asserted his concern with Russian history, in his films and in his public statements alike. 'Historical time for me has an almost physiological character. Present time I feel less.'[8] In his early works in the 1970s Mikhalkov tended to idealise Russian and Soviet history. For him, Bolshevism is an ideal and just system, underpinned by camaraderie, trust and honesty, by a genuine desire to share everything. Such a presentation of the Soviet past was suitable for the 1970s, but had to be modified after the collapse of the Soviet Union and its values. Mikhalkov responded to the changed system with expediency. Now, Stalin was disclosed as a false father figure, who betrayed and deprived the individual of responsibility for history, thereby destroying socialism. The Bolshevik remained a just man.

As Tatiana Moskvina has pointed out, in the majority of Mikhalkov's early oeuvre fatherlessness reigns.[9] With the impossibility of finding a suitable father figure in Soviet history, Mikhalkov turns to pre-Revolutionary Russia and glorifies a reactionary ruler who held the country under a firm grip. Mikhalkov cast himself in the role of three father figures in his films of the 1990s: the real father of Anna, the figure of Kotov, and Tsar Alexander III. Mikhalkov asserts the need for a father figure and a strong ruler, while his faith in Russian values and its superiority has an essentially female character, associated with mother nature and his own mother, Natalia Konchalovskaya. Mikhalkov revises history and ultimately casts himself as the father of the nation in *The Barber*, in a logical conclusion. Thus, Mikhalkov's return to the past and assertion of a strong father figure run along a vertical organisation of power that essentially contradicts the contemporary trends of new Russian cinema, which orients itself on a horizontal axis, dwelling on the theme of brotherhood as exemplified by Balabanov's *Brother* [Brat, 1997] and *Brother 2* [Brat 2, 2000] and by the popular Russian crime serials on television.

Space and Time

In defining Russia's role in history, historians and philosophers have explored Russia's geographical location between Europe and Asia, between East and West. Berdiayev in *The Russian Idea* comes down in the middle of these binary positions, defining Russia's role as the unique mediator, the bridge between two opposing philosophies of life, harbouring a dichotomy without resolving it.[10] Mikhalkov explores in his films the relation between East and West, Europe and Asia. In his early films he insisted on the Central Asian and Eastern regions being part of the Soviet empire and playing an active role in the building of socialism. In the late 1970s he began to sense the force of the land as harbouring a national idea (*Mechanical Piano* and *Oblomov*) and offering a permanence of values associated with the past. Both films advocate the impossibility of characters changing, in the same way as moral standards do not change and nor does the countryside. Mikhalkov sees changes taking place nevertheless: neither Stolz nor Petrin are condemned for their belief in progress; both are benevolent and turn a blind eye to the ultimate inability of the old guard to change.

Mikhalkov's view of the city is influenced both by his adoration for the countryside, and by a genuine nationalism (in the Slavophile tradition), which, as Gellner has noted, tied the return to national roots to the popular traditions upheld in rural areas.[11] Sofia (*Mechanical Piano*) studies in St Petersburg, but all she has learnt is words; effectively she does nothing. Romano's St Petersburg is a city reigned over by inactivity and indecision: he cannot get anyone to sign his travel permit. Oblomov's St Petersburg is a city with stifling conventions and social façades. In *Kinfolk* Moscow features as a modern city where people are content with their lot as long as they can be in the capital, even if relationships fail because of cramped living conditions. Mikhalkov depicts the city as a den of civilisation and progress that has a detrimental effect on the family, moral values and traditions. Urban culture is usually associated with art – from high culture to popular entertainment – that is, overall, presented in a negative light. Art is an influence from the West; it is an artificial rendering of emotions, perceptions and ideas which are reflected much better in nature.

Russian nature is beautiful. It is worthy of preservation and protection, and embodies all the positive values that go with his idea of a Russia of the past. A similar defence is made of the Asian steppe, which is seen as a pre-Russian landscape. Indeed, whether Mikhalkov defends nature against progress and industrialisation, or whether his lingering shots of the fields and the river are signs of a nationalistic position, is arguable. Mikhalkov's concern is the harmony of man and the past, recreated in his own cinematic mythology of Russian history.[12] In Mikhalkov's myth of Russian history the Civil War is a period of adventures in the style of a Western, or, at best, the backdrop for a romantic melodrama. The purges prevent a love story. The late nineteenth century is a paradise, threatened by progress and Western art, but not seriously in danger.

Mikhalkov's love affair with Bolshevism ended with the collapse of socialism, and has speeded up his return on screen to his real love, nineteenth-century Russia. His obsession with Russia as the motherland gave way to the narrative about the fatherland, and took a more didactic form when he exported his glorification of Russia: 'You have to have your roots in your native land, and with the branches embrace the world.'[13] Mikhalkov's view of Russia has become expansionist, and he wishes to use the medium of film to spread nineteenth-century Russian values to the world. This megalomania is what causes controversy over his public appearance and actions, and what makes him more and more controversial as didacticism prevails over his concern with film aesthetics. His image as a spiritual father contradicts his conduct as a playboy in the West.

> I have never felt a Soviet man. I am Russian. I never knew what Soviet nationality meant, this artificially constructed ideological concept, a concept that had neither roots nor a historical justification.[14]

Mikhalkov's revisionism of a lost past may not be new, but his outlook on the past largely coincided with accepted Soviet themes until the time of perestroika. His mythologising of the Revolution and the Civil War in *Slave* and *At Home Among Strangers*, his assessment of the war as a disruption that changed the life of heroes, that demanded a sacrifice (rewarded in the end in *Five Evenings*) and his farce on the inactivity of the dying class of landowners in *Mechanical Piano* were all well within the confines of the official view of the past. Plakhov is quite right when he points at the break beginning with *Oblomov*: here, Mikhalkov goes beyond the officially accepted interpretation by showing not only Stolz as a man of action in a favourable light, but also the 'Russian soul' of the conservative Oblomov. *Kinfolk* condemns progress outright. However, by claiming never to have believed in Soviet ideals Mikhalkov makes a statement that does not tally with the concern of his films. Although the theme of a glorified past is always there, it is only with *Oblomov* that the reference point is clearly and unambiguously Russia. In this sense, *Anna* is a document of falsification, where Mikhalkov betrays Soviet values in commenting on the negative effect of Soviet education on his child. Moreover, he made this film at the same time as he defended Soviet values in a speech about the management of the Film-makers' Union in 1986.[15]

Mikhalkov may hold revisionist values, he may cherish an idealised past, he may always look for the human emotions at stake in any given historical period. But what is more important is the discrepancy between the views of his films and his attempts to act in the present according to the values upheld in a mythologised past. It would seem that this is the crux of the assessment of Mikhalkov the film-maker and public figure.

Mikhalkov is clearly one of the most important and well-known Soviet and Russian film-makers. In his work, over 30 years, he has worked in a number of genres, ranging from adventure films in the Western style, melodramas, literary adaptations, screened theatre and semi-documentaries to epics. He has explored a variety of themes of universal significance, such as the responsibility of the individual towards others, towards the country, towards the environment, towards history. His films cover a variety of historical periods, from the nineteenth century to the present day. He has acted, scripted and produced, and he has taken on a variety of functions in the public sphere in recent years. He has received major national (state prize) and international (Oscar) awards and prizes at top European film festivals.

But Mikhalkov is also a controversial figure. His views on Russia were once on the verge of dissidence, advocating a return to Russia's roots at a time when Russian traditions were being 'Sovietised'. Yet, at the same time, these early images of the Russian countryside as a land that harbours values bear a mythological character rather than an authentic one. The Russia of the past is idealised, but this is done by way of a distortion of the correlation between time and space. Mikhalkov's ultimate image of Mother Russia lies in the green fields and woods, with a river quietly flowing through a valley. But this image does not exist in real time (the past), nor is it acknowledged as such by the characters in their discourse as a document or flashback, which would create an authentic relation of time and space. Rather, the image of the fields is both in the past *and* the present. Mikhalkov dissolves and blurs time and space, creating the illusion of a continuous past and, by implication, of Russia's permanence.

For Mikhalkov the image of Mother Russia – the child in the field with a river flowing quietly through a valley – is indestructible because it belongs to the past while failing to acknowledge the present. Mikhalkov thereby anticipates his Russian nationalism explicitly rendered in *The Barber*, his wish to return to the late nineteenth century, without realising that his version of the past is distorted and not suitable for the present. It is, I would suggest, this discrepancy that made *Dark Eyes* and *The Barber* in particular so controversial with Russian critics.

If Mikhalkov glorifies a rural Russia, it is in that image that he expresses his nationalism. The glorification of the past, of a Russia unspoilt by Western influences, unwilling to change, beautiful in its landscape, implies – by extension – a rejection of the West (*Barber, Kinfolk*), of the construct of 'civilisation' (*Kinfolk, Urga, Oblomov*), and of artificial 'high' – rather than popular – art (reflected in the pejorative notion of classical music, film and painting in *Quiet Day, Oblomov, Slave of Love*).

However, Mikhalkov weaves these comments into the overall narrative of the film, in which he never condemns an action or a character. His revisionist views became transparent only in his later films, and are not obvious on first viewing. With his last film, the long-awaited *Barber of Siberia*, Mikhalkov created a popular film at home and a flop abroad, tapping into the political mood of a Russia that, in 1999, was longing for order and strong leadership. At the same time, though, Europe abhorred the idea of nationalism in the wake of the strong right-wing political resurgence associated with politicians such as Le Pen and Berlusconi.

When Mikhalkov proclaimed in 1994 that *Burnt by the Sun* would be his last film, as he was going to run for the presidential elections,[16] he made a pertinent point: he wanted to be a public figure and not a film-maker. He had created the perfect Russian value system in the mythological past of his films, and felt the time had come to turn Russia back to the past. Therefore, *The Barber of Siberia* is a political statement rather than an artistic achievement: Mikhalkov sought to create for himself a new profile in a new Russia; but that Russia lay in the nineteenth century. Mikhalkov's recurrent problem of the discrepancy between time and space becomes obvious in this film. Yet, while wishing a return to the past, with all its high moral values, Mikhalkov – living not in 1885 but in 1999 – meddled in political and commercial structures while promoting his film, so that, ultimately, this latter-day Tsar Alexander III branded perfume and vodka labels while trying to be a father figure for the nation. These images did not go together. It was not, in my view, one or the other but, rather, the combination of two mutually exclusive positions that hampered Mikhalkov's image as a film-maker and a public figure.

Since 1999, Mikhalkov has not broached any new film projects, although he has occasionally, mentioned plans for a sequel to *Burnt by the Sun*.

Notes

Chapter 1

1 *Maria's Lovers* [1984], *Runaway Train* [1985], *Duet for One* [1987], *Shy People* [1988], *Homer & Eddie* [1989], *Tango & Cash* [1989], *The Inner Circle* [Blizhnii krug; Russia/Italy/United States, 1991], *The Odyssey* [1997] and *The Royal Way* [2000].

2 Mikhail Romm (1901–1971), film-maker and pedagogue at the VGIK. He made the two-part film series *Lenin in October* and *Lenin in 1918* [Lenin v oktiabre, Lenin v 1918, 1937–1939]; *The Secret Mission* [Sekretnaia missiia, 1950]; *The Russian Question* [Russkii vopros, 1948]; *Nine Days of a Year* [Deviat' dnei odnogo goda, 1962]; and *Ordinary Fascism* [Obyknovennyi fashizm, 1966]. His students include Tengiz Abuladze, Grigori Chukhrai, Vasili Shukshin, Gleb Panfilov and Georgi Daneliya.

3 The *Fitil'* ('Fuse') films were approximately five minutes long and dealt with issues of social conduct. Mikhalkov made in 1970 'Kind Words' [Dorogie slova, no. 94], 'Spoon of Tar' [Lozhka degtia, no.97] ('lozhka degtia v bochke meda' is, literally, 'a spoon of tar in a jar of honey': 'a fly in the ointment'), and 'The Unconscious' [Ne soznatel'nyi, no.98]; in 1972 'The Victims of Hospitality' [Zhertva gostopriimstva, no.125]; and in 1974 'The Object-Lesson' [Nagliadnyi urok, no.148] and 'We Begin a New Life' [Nachnem novuiu zhizn', no.150]. All these short films were made at Mosfilm under the general direction of Sergei Mikhalkov.

4 Birgit Beumers, *Burnt by the Sun*, London, 2000.

5 Metropolit Antony, *About Pushkin*, 1991; *The Affair of the Metropolit Veniamin, Petrograd 1922*, 1991; V.A. Ilyin, *About Russia*, 1991; A. Denikin, A. von Lampe, *Tragedy of the White Army*, 1992; Sasha Cherny, *Live Alphabet. Colourings*, 1992; *History of the Fatherland in Testimonies and Documents: XVIII–XX centuries*, 6 vol, 1991–1994. All published by Rossiiskii arkhiv, Moscow.

6 'Tovarishchestvo' as a company, as the word was used in the early post-Soviet years, e.g. in 'Tovarishchestvo ogranichennoi otvetstvennosti', or 'Limited Company'.

7 Boris Nemtsov (b. 1959), from 1991–1994 head of the Nizhny Novgorod administration, from 1995 governor of the Nizhny Novgorod region. In 1997–1998 first

deputy, then chairman, of the Russian government; resigned in 1998. Since 1998 leader of the party 'Rossiia molodaia' ('Young Russia'), and since 1999 head of the 'Soiuz pravykh sil' (SPS, 'Union of Right Forces').
8   See *Sovetskaia kul'tura*, 10 September 1987.
9   Zurab Tsereteli (b. 1938), president of the Russian Academy of Arts and honorary ambassador for UNESCO.
10 Alexander Vladimirovich Rutskoi (b. 1947), army general who fought in the Afghan War, and in June 1991 became vice-president of the Russian Federation. Rutskoi was suspended from duty in September 1993 when he declared himself acting president and stormed the Mayor's office and the television centre. He was subsequently removed from office and arrested under the criminal code, but released under an amnesty in 1994.
11 Sergei Mikhailovich Shakhrai (b. 1956), deputy chairman of the Russian government from April 1994 to January 1996; since October 1993 leader of the 'Partiia rossiiskogo edinstva i soglasiia' (PRES, 'Party of Russian Unity and Consent').
12 Viktor Stepanovich Chernomyrdin (b. 1938), Prime Minister from 1992 until 1998; serves on the management board of Gazprom.
13 Compare to Lord Puttnam's suggestions for the rescue of the European film industry to the Club of European Producers in December 1993 (David Puttnam, *The Undeclared War*, London, 1997, p.341) and to the structures of the French National Centre for Cinematography (CNC) discussed in Angus Finney, *The State of European Cinema*, London, 1996, pp.114–138.
14 Nikita Mikhalkov's speech to the Fourth Congress has been published (in excerpts) in the *Bulletin of the Gorky Studio* [Kinostudiia Gor'kogo: *Informatsionnyi biulleten'*], no.21 (37), 3 June 1998, pp.6–7 and, with other proceedings and reactions to the Congress, under the title 'Um i vlast', sila i mudrost'...' in *Iskusstvo kino* 8 (1998), pp.5–25.
15 'Nikita Mikhalkov: Vechny ne pamiatniki, vechen trud mastera', interview with Liudmila Semina, *Rossiiskaia gazeta*, 24 October 1997.

Chapter 2

1   Boris Shchukin (1894–1938), actor who worked with director Evgeni Vakhtangov. The Shchukin School is known for training actors in a carnivalesque and playful exploration of their roles.
2   Daneliya had made *Splendid Days* [Serezha, 1960] and *The Road to Berth* [Put' k prichalu, 1962] before casting Mikhalkov.
3   See Tatiana Moskvina, 'Nikita Mikhalkov v shutku i vser'ez,' *Iskusstvo kino* 4 (1987), pp.77–85.
4   Natalia Arinbasarova (b. 1946), played Altynai in *The First Teacher* [Pervyi uchitel', 1965]; Manshuk Mamitova in *Song about Manshuk* [Pesn' o Manshuk, 1969]; and Aizhan in *Trans-Siberian Express*, 1977.
5   Sergei Nikonenko (b. 1941), actor. Roles include Sergei Bystriakov in *Wings* [Kryl'ia, 1966]; Sinitsyn in *The Theme* [Tema, 1979]; and Yakov in *An Unfinished Piece for a Mechanical Piano*.
6   Alexander Kaidanovsky (1946–1995), graduated from the Shchukin School in 1969 and as director from VGIK in 1984. Played the title role in Tarkovsky's *Stalker* [1979]. Yuri Bogatyrev (1947–1989), graduated from the Shchukin

School in 1971, then actor at the Sovremennik Theatre (1971–1977) and later at the Moscow Arts Theatre. Roles include Maksakov in *Slave of Love*; Sergei Voinitsev in *Mechanical Piano*; Stolz in *Oblomov*; Stasik in *Kinfolk*. Alexander Porokhovshchikov (b. 1939), graduated from the Shchukin School in 1966 and worked at the Taganka and Pushkin Theatres, Moscow.

7   Cheka (Extraordinary Committee, also VChK), established 1918 by Felix Dzerzhinsky; from 1922 OGPU (State Political Directorate), from 1934 NKVD (People's Commissariat for Internal Affairs) and from 1954 KGB (Committee for State Security); disbanded 1991 and reorganised into the FSB (Federal Security Service).

8   Iurii Khaniutin, 'Rezhissura – eto professiia', in *Nikita Mikhalkov: Sbornik*, Moscow, 1989 [hereafter referred to as *Sbornik*], p.31.

9   'Our great-granddad decided to build a large boat for his great-grandchildren, and he built it all his life, but great-granddad did not finish it and left it to our granddad. We waited for this boat, which was never completed. Our father decided to build a large boat for his grandchildren, and he spent all his life building it. We dreamt about that boat and how we would sail around the world in it, but our dreams were blown away. Our dreams, our dreams.... We started building an entire ship! My son, the day will come when you will wake up in this ship, and you will stand on the deck, facing the ocean of life. Our dreams will come true in you. A ship has become of great-grandfather's boat. Here is our pride, sailing freely and unafraid of storms. My son, be worthy of our banner, goodwill and honesty. Take my faith in your happiness with you on your journey: the ship will reach all people.'

10 Alexander Kaliagin (b. 1942), worked at the Sovremennik and Moscow Arts Theatres before setting up his own theatre, 'Et Cetera', in 1993. Chairman of the Russian Theatre Union (STD).

11 Anatoli Solonitsyn (1934–1982), actor. Starred in Tarkovsky's *Andrei Rublev* and played Sartorius in *Solaris*.

12 See V. Ivanova and V. Mikhalkovich, 'Romantika prostranstva', *Sbornik*, pp.155–156.

13 Elena Stishova, 'Snimaetsia kino', *Iskusstvo kino* 4 (1977), pp.94–103.

14 Iurii Bogomolov, 'Svoi sredi chuzhikh...', *Sbornik*, p.142.

15 A. Troshin, 'V svoem zhanre', *Literaturnaia Rossiia*, 22 November 1974.

16 A. Iuren'ev, 'Romantika bor'by', *Sovetskaia kul'tura*, 1 April 1975.

17 Svetlana Boym, *Common Places*, Cambridge, MA, and London, 1994, pp.283–291; and *The Future of Nostalgia*, New York, 2002, Introduction and part 1.

18 This scene is, in its choreography, somewhat reminiscent of the procession of the 'tsarevna' in Khamdamov's original film.

19 Ivan Mosjoukine [Mozzhukhin] (1890–1939), actor of silent film. Emigrated to Paris in 1920, where he was closely associated with Albatros studios, an enclave of Russian émigré film-makers in the French film industry.

20 Joan Neuberger, 'Between Public and Private: Revolution and Melodrama in Nikita Mikhalkov's *Slave of Love*', in *Imitations of Life: Two Centuries of Melodrama in Russia*, ed. Louise McReynolds and Joan Neuberger, Durham and London, 2002, pp.259–282.

21 Neuberger, p.266.

22 'Where are you, dream? Where are you, dream? With hope I look into the distance and a fine sound comes to me in the fragile silence. Is it laughter? No,

it is you, love. Somebody's heavy heart, somebody's burning glance, if only a precious word could be said, and open the soul... not to thunders and storms, but to a light breeze. Not to friendship, but only to love. My soul, warm it in your palms. I believe in you, I believe in the dream, I believe in love. Yes, I believe in love and that it will come.'

23 Neuberger, p.281.
24 A. Lipkov, 'Istoriia liubvi, istoriia vremeni', *Pravda*, 18 June 1976.
25 Stishova, 'Snimaetsia kino', p.96.
26 Boym, *Common Places*, p.284.
27 Birgit Beumers, 'The Soviet and Russian Blockbuster: A Question of Genre?', *Slavic Review*, vol. 62, no. 3 (Fall 2003), pp.441–454.
28 Neuberger, p.263.
29 Stishova, 'Snimaetsia kino', p.96.
30 Shaken Aimanov (1914–1970), Kazakh actor and film-maker, director of the Kazakh theatre in Alma-Ata (1947–1951). The Kazakh film studio in Almaty was named after him (1984).
31 Asanali Ashimov (b. 1939), works at Kazakhfilm and has become best known for his parts as Chadiarov-Fan-Isidzima in the trilogy.
32 OGPU – Soviet secret service; see note 7 above.

Chapter 3

1 Boym, *Common Places*, pp.284–287.
2 Edward Braun, 'From Platonov to Piano', in *The Cambridge Companion to Chekhov*, ed. Vera Gottlieb and Paul Allain, Cambridge, 2000, pp.43–56.
3 Margarita Kvasnetskaia, 'Schet s sovest'iu', *Sovetskii fil'm* 5 (1977), pp.13–15.
4 Zinovii Papernyi, 'Granitsy smeshnogo', *Literaturnaia gazeta*, 14 September 1977.
5 Anna Lawton, *Kinoglasnost*, Cambridge, 1992, p.27.
6 Lawton, p.27.
7 Aleksandr Svobodin, 'Vol'nyi Chekhov', *Iskusstvo kino* 10 (1977), pp.121–136.
8 Svobodin, p.123.
9 See Kvasnetskaia, 'Schet s sovest'iu'.
10 Kvasnetskaia, 'Schet s sovest'iu', p.15.
11 Iurii Khaniutin, 'Rezhisser, eto professiia', *Sovetskaia kul'tura*, 7 June 1977.
12 Maia Turovskaia, 'Kino – Chekhov 77 – teatr', *Iskusstvo kino* 1 (1978), p.104.
13 See Anatoly Smeliansky, *The Russian Theatre after Stalin*, Cambridge, 1999, pp.50–52.
14 The song is 'Guby okaiannye' by Yuli Kim: 'Damned lips, secret thoughts, confusion of love. Confusion of love, desperate fellow. All you lips, remember! All you thoughts, you know how sad you make my heart with this. I lure the dove, the blue-grey bird. I send you a letter, and we begin all over again; I send you a letter, and we begin all over again.'
15 Liudmila Gurchenko (b. 1935), graduated from VGIK. Played Lena Krylova in *Carnival Night* [Karnaval'naia noch', 1956] and numerous roles in popular musical comedies. Stanislav Liubshin (b. 1933), graduated from the Maly Theatre's Shchepkin School in 1959, and worked at various Moscow theatres before joining the Moscow Arts Theatre in 1981.
16 See Iuren'ev, 'Piat' vecherov i dva aktera', *Sovetskaia kul'tura*, 3 August 1979.

17 Elena Stishova, 'Piat' vecherov i vsia zhizn'', *Iskusstvo kino* 10 (1979): p.48
18 Boym, *The Future of Nostalgia*, p.xviii.
19 See Varshavskii, 'Reabilitatsiia idealov', *Sbornik*, p.13.
20 Stishova, 'Piat' vecherov i vsia zhizn'', p.44.
21 Dobroliubov, 'What is Oblomovshchina?' (1859).
22 Oleg Tabakov (b. 1937), graduated from the Moscow Arts Theatre School in 1957 and founded, with Oleg Efremov, the Sovremennik Theatre. In 1983 he joined the Moscow Arts Theatre, the artistic director of which he became after Efremov's death in 2000. Tabakov founded his own theatre in 1986.
23 Andrei Popov (1918–1983), artistic director of the Central Theatre of the Red Army (1963–1974), actor at the Moscow Arts Theatre (1974–1983) and professor of the Theatre Institute (GITIS).
24 Latin: a sane mind in a healthy body.
25 Neia Zorkaia, 'Dni Oblomova', *Sovetskaia Rossiia*, 10 June 1980.
26 Andrei Plakhov, 'Postizhenie ili adaptatsiia', *Iskusstvo kino* 6 (1980), p.64.
27 V. Ivanova and V. Mikhalkovich, 'Romantika prostranstva', *Sbornik*, p.161.
28 Boym, *Common Places*, pp.283–291, and *The Future of Nostalgia*.
29 See Birgit Beumers, 'Literary heritage as lens: the Mikhalkov Brothers' view of Russia', conference paper, University of Surrey, May 2002. Forthcoming as 'The Mikhalkov Brothers' View of Russia', in S. Hutchings and A. Vernitski (eds), *Film Adaptations of Literature in Russia and the Soviet Union 1917–2001*, London, 2004.
30 Inna Vishnevskaia, 'Geroi i negeroi Goncharova', *Sovetskii ekran* 6 (1980).
31 See Russell Valentino, 'Adapting the landscape: Oblomov's vision in film', conference paper, University of Surrey, May 2002.
32 Valentino, p.13.
33 Boym, *Common Places*, p.284.

Chapter 4

1 Oleg Menshikov (b. 1960), graduated in 1982 from the Shchepkin Theatre School. Worked as actor in several Moscow theatres (Soviet Army Theatre, Ermolova Theatre) and has directed his own theatre productions. Roles in film include Mitia in *Burnt by the Sun* [1994]; Sasha Kostylin in *The Prisoner of the Mountains* [Kavkazskii plennik, 1996]; Andrei Tolstoy in *The Barber of Siberia* [Sibirskii tsiriul'nik, 1998].
2 Vladimir Ilyin (b. 1947), graduated from the Sverdlovsk Theatre Institute. Worked at the Mayakovsky Theatre, Moscow from 1974–1989. Roles include Sedov in *Defence Counsel Sedov* [Zashchitnik Sedov, 1988] and Kirik in *Burnt by the Sun* [Utomlennye solntsem, 1994].
3 Nonna (Noiabrina) Mordiukova (b. 1925), studied at VGIK. Appeared in *Young Guard* [Molodaia gvardiia, 1949], and played Vavilova in Askoldov's *The Commissar* [Komissar, 1967, released 1987].
4 Dmitri and Vladimir Shlapentokh argue that the music is a manifestation of bad Western influence (*Soviet Cinematography 1918–1991*, New York, 1993, p.161). I disagree with this view, as it oversimplifies the matter.
5 Armen Medvedev suggests the images of the runner and the aircraft as dividers, without however relating them to Afghanistan. I have extended his division and

interpretation here. Medvedev, 'Voprosy posle fil'ma', *Iskusstvo kino* 3 (1983), pp.22–37.
6   Mikhail Ul'ianov, 'S bol'iu o rodne', *Sovetskaia Rossiia*, 5 October 1982.
7   Eduard Artem'ev, 'Dukhovnoe prostranstvo', *Sbornik*, p.173.
8   See Lev Anninskii, 'Pereplias na pereput'e', *Sbornik*, p.113.
9   Irina Kupchenko, (b. 1948), graduated from the Shchukin School. Roles include Kalitina in *A Nest of Gentlefolk* [Dvorianskoe gnezdo, 1969]; Sonia in *Uncle Vania* [Diadia Vania, 1971]. Mikhail Ulianov (b. 1927), graduated from the Shchukin School as actor; since 1987 director of the Vakhtangov Theatre. Known for his parts of Lenin (e.g. in *On the Path to Lenin* [Na puti k Leninu, 1970]); and Zhukov (e.g. in *Liberation*; [Osvobozhdenie, 1968–1971]; *Choice of Target* [Vybor tseli, 1974]; *The Blockade* [Blokada, 1974]; *Battle for Moscow* [Bitva za Moskvu, 1985]; *Stalingrad* [1989]; and *The Law* [Zakon, 1989]).

Chapter 5

1   See Lawton, *Kinoglasnost*, pp.52–69.
2   Gillo Dorfles, 'Myth and Kitsch', in Gillo Dorfles (ed.) *Kitsch: An Anthology of Bad Taste*, London: Studio Vista, 1969, p.43.
3   Boym, *Common Places*, p.287.
4   Dorfles, 'Myth and Kitsch', pp.37–48.
5   Dorfles distinguishes between mythogogic (a myth that instructs) and mythopoetic (a myth that creates), compulsory and creative myth making (p.37).
6   Gilles Deleuze, *Cinema 2: The Time-Image*, London, 1989, p.126.
7   Tatiana Moskvina, 'La Grande Illusion', in *Russia on Reels*, Birgit Beumers (ed.), London, 1999, p.104.
8   Pavel Lebeshev, 'Sotrudnichestvo', *Sbornik*, p.195; Galina Orekhanova, 'Posle vtorogo prishestviia', *Sovetskaia Rossiia*, 1 September 1994.
9   'Ochi chernye', *Sovetskaia kul'tura*, 23 November 1989.
10 Ts. Kobrinskaia, 'Arbuz i sobachka', *Sovetskaia kul'tura*, 3 November 1988.
11 A. Lepshei, 'Vysyvaet nedoumenie', *Sovetskaia kul'tura*, 24 December 1988.
12 Nina Agisheva, 'Kak zhivesh', chelovek?', *Literaturnoe obozrenie* 9 (1987), p.87.
13 Andrey Tarkovsky, *Sculpting in Time*, Austin, 1986, pp.213 and 216.
14 L. Strel'kov, 'Territoriia liubvi – blizhnii krug?', *Pravda*, 15 April 1993.
15 Petr Vail', 'Potomok Chingis-khana', *Nezavisimaia gazeta*, 26 November 1992.
16 Aleksandr Genis, 'Bremia belogo cheloveka', *Nezavisimaia gazeta*, 26 November 1992.
17 See Andrei Plakhov, 'Russkii dukh za kitaiskoi stenoi', *Iskusstvo kino* 2 (1992): pp.83–89.
18 Vail', 'Potomok Chingis-khana'.
19 Andrei Plakhov, 'Postmodernism s chelovecheskim litsom', *Moskovskie novosti* 39 (1991).
20 Plakhov, 'Russkii dukh...', p.84.

Chapter 6

1. Birgit Beumers, 'Cinemarket, or the Russian Film Industry in "Mission Possible"', *Europe-Asia-Studies* vol. 51, no.5, 1999, pp.871–896.
2. For a discussion of the 'Russian idea', see Beumers (ed.), *Russia on Reels*.
3. The crocodile Gena features in the stories of the children's writer Eduard Uspensky, which form the scripts for one of the most popular animated films.
4. Caretaker-singer: as the Soviet Citizen's Codex stipulated that everybody had to work, and jazz and rock musicians belonged to no union that would give them official status, many rock musicians worked as caretakers, often on the night shift, and performed outside their working hours unofficially.
5. Mikhalkov's voice in *Anna: Ot shesti do vosemnadtsati*, montage script (unpublished), pp.57–58.
6. Sergei Mikhalkov, 'Ia sluzhil gosudarstvu', interview with Irina Arzamastseva, *Kontinent* 96 (1998), pp.342–357.
7. See Yuri Trifonov's novel *Dom na naberezhnoi* (Moscow, 1976; English translation by Michael Glenny as *House on the Embankment*, London, 1985), set in the building at the time of the purges and during the war.
8. There are certain parallels in the plot to Arkadi Gaidai's story *The Blue Cup*.
9. Katerina Clark, *Petersburg: Crucible of Cultural Revolution*, Cambridge, MA, 1995; and Vladimir Paperny, *Kul'tura dva*, Moscow, 1996.
10. A similar scene is described in Yuri Trifonov's uncompleted novel *Ischeznovenie* (Moscow, 1987; English translation by David Lowe as *Disappearance*, Ann Arbor, 1991), where a dirigible with Stalin's portrait floats over the nocturnal Moscow.
11. For a full discussion of the elements of the game see Kulish's review translated in Beumers, *Burnt by the Sun*.
12. See Louis Menashe's review in *Cineaste* XXI, no. 4 (1995), pp.43–44.
13. Leonid Pavliuchik, interview, 'Nikita Mikhalkov, utomlennyi kinoprokatom', *Izvestiia*, 26 January 1995.
14. See Shlapentokh, *Soviet Cinematography*, p.161.
15. Moskvina, 'La Grande Illusion', p.93.
16. Nikita Mikhalkov, 'Rezhisser ne dolzhen dolgo nakhodit'sia pod obaianiem svoei kartiny. Eto opasno', *Iskusstvo kino* 3 (1995), pp.9–13.
17. Kalatozov won the Golden Palm for *The Cranes are Flying*, a film about the effect of the war on ordinary people.
18. For a full discussion of the film and its reception see Beumers, *Burnt by the Sun*.
19. T. Moskvina, 'Mikhalkov' in *SEANS-Kinoslovar: Noveishaia istoriia otechestvennogo kino 1986–2000*, vol. 2, St Petersburg, 2001, pp.282–285.
20. For a full account of these inaccuracies see Nikita Sokolov, 'Slav'sia great Russia...', *Itogi*, 9 March 1999, pp.48–49.
21. For a full analysis of the historical inaccuracies, especially relating to the military history, see Aleksandr Kiborskii, *Sibirskii tsiriul'nik. Pravda i vymysel kinoepopei*, Moscow, 2002.
22. See Chapter 1, note 14.
23. N. Sokolov, 'Slav'sia ...', p.49.
24. *Itogi*, 9 March 1999, p.41.
25. N. Sokolov, 'Slav'sia ...', p.49.

Concluding Remarks

1. Alexander Adabashian (b. 1945), graduated from the Stroganov Institute for Art.
2. Vladimir Aronin (b. 1941), graduated from VGIK in 1969.
3. Pavel Lebeshev (1940–2003), son of the DoP Timofei Lebeshev (1905–1981), graduated from VGIK in 1972.
4. Neia Zorkaia, 'Pavel Lebeshev', booklet for the Moscow Film Festival, 2000.
5. V. Ivanova, V. Mikhalkovich, 'Romantika prostranstva', *Sbornik*, p.161.
6. Eduard Artemiev (b. 1937), graduated from the Moscow Conservatory; the first composer to use electronic music in film.
7. Georgii Daneliia, 'Chuvstvuia vzgliad druga...', *Sbornik*, pp.20–28.
8. N. Mikhalkov in an interview with A. Nitochkina, 'Mechty etogo cheloveka', *Iskusstvo kino* 6 (1989), p.31.
9. Moskvina, 'La Grande Illusion'.
10. Nicholas Berdyaev, *The Russian Idea*, London, 1947.
11. Ernest Gellner, *Nationalism*, London, 1997, pp.81–82.
12. 'Mechty etogo cheloveka', p.33.
13. 'Mechty etogo cheloveka', p.39.
14. N. Mikhalkov, 'Ia snimaiu o tom, chto liubliu', *Iskusstvo kino* 2 (1992), p.89.
15. See Lawton, *Kinoglasnost*, chapter 2.
16. Vitalii Grigor'ev, 'N. Mikhalkov: Belyi orel na krasnom pole', http://www.whoiswho.ru/russian/Free/51998/mihalkovr.htm [accessed 4/7/02].

Filmography

1. Mikhalkov: Actor – Scriptwriter – Producer

Films are listed here in chronological order.

Actor

The Sun Shines for All (*The Sun Shines for Everybody*) [Solntse svetit vsem, 1959], dir. K. Voinov
Clouds Over Borsk [Tuchi nad Borskom, 1960], dir. V. Ordynsky
The Adventures of Krosh [Prikliucheniia Krosha, 1961], dir. G. Oganisian: Vadim
I Walk Around Moscow (*Meet Me in Moscow*) [Ia shagaiu po Moskve, 1963], dir. G. Daneliya: Kolka
Roll-Call [Pereklichka, 1965], dir. D. Khrabrovitsky: Sergei Borodin
Year as Long as Life [God, kak zhizn', 1965], dir. G. Roshal': Jules
A Small Joke [Shutochka, 1966] (TV), dir. A. Smirnov: young man
Not the Luckiest Day [Ne samyi udachnyi den', 1966], dir. Yu. Egorov: Nikita
The Red and the White [Csillagosok, katonák, 1967], dir. M. Jancsó: White officer
War and Peace [1965, 1968] (uncredited)
Song About Manshuk [Pesn' o Manshuk, 1969], dir. M. Belagin: Lieutenant Ezhov
A Nest of Gentlefolk [Dvorianskoe gnezdo, 1969], dir. A. Konchalovsky: Count Nelidov
Sport, Sport, Sport [1970], dir. E. Klimov
The Red Tent [Krasnaia palatka, 1971], dir. M. Kalatozov: Chuknovsky, icebreaker pilot
Hold On to the Clouds [Derzhis' za oblaka, 1971], dir. Boris Grigoriev: Peter Szasz
The Stationmaster [Stantsionnyi smotritel', 1972] (TV), dir. S. Soloviev: Captain Minsky
At Home Among Strangers, a Stranger at Home [Svoi sredi chuzhikh, chuzhoi sredi svoikh, 1974]: Brylov

Slave of Love [Raba liubvi, 1975]: Ivan
An Unfinished Piece for a Mechanical Piano (*An Unfinished Piece for a Player Piano*) [Neokonchennaia p'esa dlia mekhanicheskogo pianino, 1977]: Nikolai Ivanovich Triletsky
Siberiade [Sibiriada, 1978], dir. A. Konchalovsky: Aleksei Ustiuzhanin
Kinfolk (*Family Relations*) [Rodnia, 1981]: waiter
The Hound of the Baskervilles [Prikliucheniia Sherloka Kholmsa i doktora Vatsona: Sobaka Baskervilei, 1981] (TV), dir. I. Maslennikov: Sir Henry Baskerville
Portrait of the Artist's Wife [Portret zheny khudozhnika, 1981], dir. A. Pankratov: Boris Petrovich
Two Voices [Dva golosa, 1981] (TV), dir. A. Belinsky: main role
A Railway Station for Two [Vokzal dlia dvoikh, 1982], dir. E. Riazanov: Andrei
Dream Flights (*Flights in Dreams and in Reality; Flights of Fancy*) [Polety vo sne i naiavu, 1982], dir. R. Balaian: director
The Traffic Officer [Inspektor GAI, 1982], dir. E. Urazbaev: Trunov
250 Grammes: A Radioactive Testament [250 grammaa – radioaktiivinen testamentti, 1983], dir. Pirho Honkasalo: father
A Cruel Romance [Zhestokii romans, 1984], dir. E. Riazanov: Sergei Sergeevich Paratov
Aurora (*Under Northern Lights*) [Pod severnym siianiem, 1990], dirs Petras Abukiavičius, Tosio Goto: Lezhnev
The Insulted and Injured [Unizhennye i oskorblennye, 1990], dir. A. Eshpai: Valkovsky
Urga: Close to Eden [Urga, 1991]: cyclist (uncredited)
A Beautiful Stranger [Piękna nieznajoma, 1992], dir. Jerzy Hoffmann: the colonel
Anna from Six to Eighteen [Anna: Ot shesti do vosemnadtsati, 1993]: Himself
Burnt by the Sun [Utomlennye solntsem, 1994]: Colonel Sergei Kotov
A Time to Love and a Time to Hate [Vremia liubit' i vremia nenavidet', 1994]: Himself
The Government Inspector [Revizor, 1996], dir. Sergei Gazarov: Mayor
The Barber of Siberia [Sibirskii tsiriul'nik, 1998]: Alexander III
Belief, Hope and Blood [Vera, nadezhda, krov', 2000], dir. Marina Dubrovina

Scriptwriter

Risk [1970], dir. Vasile Pescaru
At Home Among Strangers, a Stranger at Home [Svoi sredi chuzhikh, chuzhoi sredi svoikh, 1974]
Hatred [Nenavist', 1975], dir. Samvel Gasparov
Trans-Siberian Express [Transsibirskii ekspress, 1977], dir. Eldor Urazbayev
An Unfinished Piece for a Mechanical Piano (*An Unfinished Piece for a Player Piano*) [Neokonchennaia p'esa dlia mekhanicheskogo pianino, 1977]
Five Evenings [Piat' vecherov, 1978]
A Few Days from the Life of I.I. Oblomov [Neskol'ko dnei iz zhizni I.I. Oblomova, 1979]
A Private Conversation (*Without Witness*) [Bez svidetelei, 1983]
My Favourite Clown [Moi liubimyi kloun, 1986], dir. Yuri Kushnerev
Dark Eyes (*Black Eyes*) [Oci ciornie, Italy, 1987]
Lonely Hunter [Martokhela monadire/Odinokii okhotnik, 1989], dir. Keti Dolidze
Urga: Close to Eden [Urga, 1992]

Anna from Six to Eighteen [Anna: Ot shesti do vosemnadtsati, 1993]
Burnt by the Sun [Utomlennye solntsem, 1994]
The Barber of Siberia [Sibirskii tsiriul'nik, 1998]

Producer

Anna from Six to Eighteen [Anna: Ot shesti do vosemnadtsati, 1993]
Burnt by the Sun [Utomlennye solntsem, 1994]
The Barber of Siberia [Sibirskii tsiriul'nik, 1998] (co-producer with Michel Seydoux)
Tender Age [Nezhnyi vozrast, 2001] dir. Sergei Soloviev

2. Films Directed by Mikhalkov: Credits

Things [Veshchi, 1967], aka *The Little Girl and Things* [Devochka i veshchi] (short)
VGIK, Masterclass Mikhail Romm

And I Go Home [A ia uezzhaiu domoi, 1968] (short)
VGIK, Masterclass Mikhail Romm
Script: Nikita Mikhalkov

A Quiet Day at the End of the War (aka *Quiet Day at War's End*) [Spokoinyi den' v kontse voiny, 1971]
Mosfilm, 38 min
Script: Rustam Ibragimbekov
Director of photography: Dmitri Korzhikhin
Composer: Eduard Artemiev
Cast
Adalat   Natalia Arinbasarova
Andrei   Sergei Nikonenko
and Lev Durov, Alexander Kaidanovsky, Yuri Bogatyrev, Alexander Porokhovshchikov

At Home Among Strangers, a Stranger at Home [Svoi sredi chuzhikh, chuzhoi sredi svoikh, 1974]
Mosfilm, 97 min (23.7 million spectators)
Script: Eduard Volodarsky, Nikita Mikhalkov
Director of photography: Pavel Lebeshev
Design: Irina Shreter, Alexander Adabashian
Composer: Eduard Artemiev (Lyrics: Natalia Konchalovskaya; Songs: Alexander Gradsky)
Cast
Egor Shilov   Yuri Bogatyrev
Committee Chairman Sarychev   Anatoli Solonitsyn
Zabelin   Sergei Shakurov
Nikolai Kungurov   Alexander Porokhovshchikov
Lipiagin   Nikolai Pastukhov
Lemke   Alexander Kaidanovsky

Brylov
Vaniukin
Kadyrkul
Festivals: IFF Delhi, 1975

Nikita Mikhalkov
Alexander Kaliagin
Konstantin Raikin

Slave of Love [Raba liubvi, 1975]
Mosfilm, 94 min (11.2 million spectators)
Script: Friedrich Gorenstein, Andrei Mikhalkov-Konchalovsky
Director of Photography: Pavel Lebeshev
Design: Alexander Adabashian, Alexander Samulekin
Composer: Eduard Artemiev
Cast
Olga Voznesenskaya
Viktor Pototsky
Alexander Kaliagin
Savva Yuzhakov
Fedotov

Elena Solovei
Rodion Nakhapetov
Alexander Kaliagin
Oleg Basilashvili
Konstantin Grigoriev

Festivals: IFF Teheran, 1976

An Unfinished Piece for a Mechanical Piano (aka *An Unfinished Piece for a Player Piano*) [Neokonchennaia p'esa dlia mekhanicheskogo pianino, 1977]
Mosfilm 103 min
Subtitled video ASIN B00004CM8O
Script: Alexander Adabashian, Nikita Mikhalkov
Director of photography: Pavel Lebeshev
Design: Alexander Adabashian, Alexander Samulekin
Composer: Eduard Artemiev
Cast
Mikhail Vasilievich Platonov
Sofia Egorovna
Sashenka (Alexandra Ivanovna Triletskaya)
Anna Petrovna Voinitseva
Sergei Pavlovich Voinitsev (her stepson)
Pavel Petrovich Shcherbuk
Porfiry Semenovich Glagoliev
Ivan Ivanovich Triletsky
Nikolai Ivanovich Triletsky (doctor)
Gerasim Kuzmich Petrin
Verochka
Lizochka
Yakov
Petia

Alexander Kaliagin
Elena Solovei
Evgeniya Glushenko
Antonina Shuranova
Yuri Bogatyrev
Oleg Tabakov
Nikolai Pastukhov
Pavel Kadochnikov
Nikita Mikhalkov
Anatoly Romashin
Natalia Nazarova
Kseniya Minina
Sergei Nikonenko
Seryozha Guriev

Festivals: IFF San Sebastian, 1977 (Grand Prix for Best Direction); Cartahan, Columbia, 1977; Chicago, 1978; 'Fest 78', Belgrade, 1978; Florence, 1978

Five Evenings [Piat' vecherov, 1978]
Mosfilm, 103 min
Script: Alexander Adabashian, Nikita Mikhalkov
Director of photography: Pavel Lebeshev

Design: Alexander Adabashian, Alexander Samulekin
Composer: Eduard Artemiev
Cast

Tamara Vasilievna	Liudmila Gurchenko
Alexander Petrovich Ilyin	Stanislav Liubshin
Zoya	Valentina Telichkina
Katia	Larisa Kuznetsova
Slava	Igor Nefedov
Timofeyev	Alexander Adabashian

Best Foreign Film in Polish and Bulgarian distribution
Festivals: Hyères, France, 1979

Oblomov (A Few Days from the Life of I.I. Oblomov) [Neskol'ko dnei iz zhizni I.I. Oblomova, 1979]
Mosfilm, 143 min (3.7 million spectators)
Script: Alexander Adabashian, Nikita Mikhalkov
Director of photography: Pavel Lebeshev
Design: Alexander Adabashian, Alexander Samulekin
Composer: Eduard Artemiev (using fragments from Bellini, Rachmaninov)
Cast

Oblomov	Oleg Tabakov
Stolz	Yuri Bogatyrev
Zakhar	Andrei Popov
Olga	Elena Solovei
Alexeyev	Avangard Leontiev
Father	Evgeni Steblov
Baron	Gleb Strizhenov
Ilya as a child	Andrei Razumovsky
Stoltz as a child	Oleg Kozlov
Katia	Elena Kleshchevskaya
Olga's aunt	Galina Shostko
Narrator	Anatoli Romashin
Oblomov's mother	Evgeniya Glushenko
Oblomov's father	Nikolai Pastukhov

Best Foreign Film (American Filmcritics, 1981)
Festivals: Oxford, 1980; Malaga, 1982

Kinfolk (aka *Family Relations*) [Rodnia, 1981]
Mosfilm, 98 min (15.2 million spectators)
Script: Viktor Merezhko
Director of photography: Pavel Lebeshev
Design: Alexander Adabashian, Alexander Samulekin
Composer: Eduard Artemiev
Cast

Maria Vasilievna Konovalova	Nonna Mordiukova
Nina	Svetlana Kriuchkova
Yuri Nikolayevich Liapin	Andrei Petrov
Konovalov	Ivan Bortnik
Stasik	Yuri Bogatyrev

General	Vsevolod Larionov
Waiter	Nikita Mikhalkov
Kirill	Oleg Menshikov
Lara	Larissa Kuznetsova
Irina	Fedia Stukov

Private Conversation (aka ***Without Witness***) [Bez svidetelei, 1983]
Mosfilm, 95 min (6.3 million spectators)
Script: Nikita Mikhalkov, Sofia Prokofieva, R Fataliev (based on Prokofieva's play)
Director of photography: Pavel Lebeshev
Design: Alexander Adabashian, I Makarov
Composer: Eduard Artemiev
Cast

She	Irina Kupchenko
He	Mikhail Ulianov

Festivals: Moscow IFF, 1983 (FIPRESCI award); Valladolid (Spain), 1984; Kiev, 1984

Dark Eyes [Oci ciornie, 1987]
Italy (Silvia d'Amico Bendico Carlo Cucchi, RAI 1, Ardiano), 121 min
Subtitled video ASIN B00004CLI2
Script: Alexander Adabashian and Nikita Mikhalkov
Director of photography: Franco di Giacomo
Design: Mario Garbulia, Alexander Adabashian
Composer: Francis Ley
Cast

Romano	Marcello Mastroianni
Elisa	Silvana Mangano
Anna	Elena Safonova
Tina	Marthe Keller
Elisa's mother	Pina Cei
Pavel Alexeyev	Vsevolod Larionov
Governor of Sisoev	Innokenti Smoktunovsky
The lawyer	Roberto Herlitzka
Manlio	Paolo Baroni
Konstantin	Dmitri Zolotukhin

Oleg Tabakov, Yuri Bogatyrev in cameo roles
Festivals: Cannes, 1987

Hitchhike (French title: ***L'Autostop***) [Avtostop, 1990]
USSR/Switzerland/Italy, 56 min
Script: Rustam Ibragimbekov
Director of photography: Franco di Giacomo
Composer: Eduard Artemiev
Design: Vladimir Aronin
Cast

Sandro	Massimo Venturiello
Nastia	Nina Ruslanova
Sasha	Vladimir Gostiukhin
Russian Officer	Stepan Mikhalkov

Urga (aka *Urga: Close to Eden*) [Urga, 1991]
France/USSR (Camera One, Hachette, TriTe, Pyramide), 120 min
Subtitled video ASIN B00004CMZJ
Script: Nikita Mikhalkov and Rustam Ibragimbekov
Director of photography: Vilen Kaliuta
Composer: Eduard Artemiev
Cast

Pagma	Badema
Gombo	Bayaertu
Sergei	Vladimir Gostiukhin
Grandma	Babouchka
Marina	Larisa Kuznetsova
Stanislas	Jon Bochinski
Burma	Yongyan Bao
Buyin	Wurinile
Van Biao	Biao Wang
Bayartu	Baoyinhexige
Nikolai	Nikolai Voschilin

Festivals: Venice IFF, 1991 (Golden Lion)
Russian Film Academy Award NIKA, 1992; Kinotavr, 1992; Russian State Prize, 1992; European Film Academy (Felix), 1993; Oscar nomination, 1993

Anna from Six to Eighteen [Anna: Ot shesti do vosemnadtsati, 1993]
Russia/France (TriTe and Camera One), 100 min
Subtitled video ASIN 1567301630 (US)
Directors of photography: Pavel Lebeshev, Elizbar Karabaev, Vadim Yusov, Vadim Alisov
Festivals: Leipzig, 1994

Burnt by the Sun (French title: *Soleil trompeur*) [Utomlennye solntsem, 1994]
Russia/France (TriTe, Camera One, Roskomkino), 151 min
(48 weeks leader in Russian video sales)
Subtitled video ASIN B00004CRNN (Pathe)
Screenplay: Nikita Mikhalkov, Rustam Ibragimbekov
Composer: Eduard Artemiev
Director of photography: Vilen Kaliuta
Design: Vladimir Aronin, Alexander Samulekin
Costumes: Natalia Ivanova
Cast

Dmitri (Mitia)	Oleg Menshikov
Sergei Petrovich Kotov	Nikita Mikhalkov
Marusia (Musia)	Ingeborga Dapkunaite
Nadia	Nadia Mikhalkova
Vsevolod Konstantinovich	Viacheslav Tikhonov
Katia Mokhova	Svetlana Kriuchkova
Kirik	Vladimir Ilyin
Lidia Stepanovna	Alla Kazanskaya
Elena Mikhailovna	Nina Arkhipova
Driver	Avangard Leontiev

Philippe	André Umansky
Olga Nikolayevna	Inna Ulianova
Liuba	Liubov Rudneva
NKVD officer	Vladimir Riabov
First NKVD man	Vladimir Belousov
Second NKVD man	Alexei Pokatilov
Lieutenant	Evgeni Mironov

Festivals: Cannes, 1994 (Grand Prix); Oscar, 1995.

The Barber of Siberia [Sibirskii tsiriul'nik, 1998]
France/Russia (TriTe, Camera One, Barandoff, France 2, Medusa), 179 min
Subtitled video ASIN B000058CB9 (Pathe)
Producer: Michel Seydoux, Nikita Mikhalkov
(France: 270,000 spectators in 1st week)
(Russia: 1st place in distribution, 2nd in video sales for 2000)
Script: Rustam Ibragimbekov, Nikita Mikhalkov
Director of photography: Pavel Lebeshev
Design: Vladimir Aronin
Costumes: N. Ivanova, Vladimir Zaitsev
Composer: Eduard Artemiev
Cast

Jane Callahan	Julia Ormond
Douglas McCracken	Richard Harris
Andrei Tolstoy	Oleg Menshikov
General Radlov	Alexei Petrenko
Tolstoy's mother	Marina Neyolova
Captain Mokin	Vladimir Ilyin
Kopnovsky	Daniel Olbrychski
Duniasha	Anna Mikhalkova
Polievsky	Marat Basharov
Alibekov	Nikita Tatarenkov
Buturlin	Artem Mikhalkov
Cadet Nazarov	Egor Dronov
Andrei's uncle	Avangard Leontiev
Forsten	Robert Hardy
Perepyolkina	Elizabeth Spriggs

Festivals: Cannes, 1999 (opening); Russian State Prize, 1999

Bibliography

Bibliographical Works and Books about Mikhalkov in Russian:

Sandler, A.M. (ed.), *Nikita Mikhalkov: Sbornik*, Moscow, 1989 [referred to in notes as as *Sbornik*].

Matizen, Viktor, (ed.), *Nikita*, Moscow, 1995.

Nikita Mikhalkov: Fil'mo- i bibliograficheskii ukazatel [Nikita Mikhalkov: Filmographical and bibliographical guide], compiled by T. Suminova. Moskva: Studiia TriTe/ Rossiiskii arkhiv, 1995. [Full list of sources of Russian and foreign reviews of Mikhalkov's work until 1995.]

Kinograf no. 4 (1997), pp.148-165. [Bibliographical apparatus on *Burnt by the Sun*.]

Publications about Mikhalkov in English:

Beumers, Birgit, *Burnt by the Sun*, Kinofile 3, London, 2000.

Beumers, Birgit, 'The Barber of Siberia', in *European Cinema*, Jill Forbes and Sarah Street (eds), London, 2000, pp.195-206.

Braun, Edward, 'From Platonov to Piano', in *The Cambridge Companion to Chekhov*, Vera Gottlieb and Paul Allain (eds), Cambridge, 2000, pp.43-56.

Gillespie, David and Natal'ia Zhuravkina, 'Nikita Mikhalkov's *Utomlennye solntsem*, *Rusistika* 13 (June 1996), pp.58-61.

Larsen, Susan, 'National Identity, Cultural Authority and the Post-Soviet Blockbuster: Nikita Mikhalkov and Aleksei Balabanov', *Slavic Review*, vol. 62, no. 3 (Fall 2003), pp.491-511.

Moskvina, Tatiana, 'La Grande Illusion', in *Russia on Reels*, Birgit Beumers (ed.), London, 1999, pp.91-104.

Neuberger, Joan, 'Between Public and Private: Revolution and Melodrama in Nikita Mikhalkov's *Slave of Love*', in *Imitations of Life: Two Centuries of Melodrama in Russia*, Louise McReynolds and Joan Neuberger (eds), Durham and London, 2002, pp.259-282.

Contemporary Russian Cinema and Culture:

Attwood, Lynne (ed.), *Red Women on the Silver Screen: Soviet Women and Cinema from the Beginning to the End of the Communist Era*, London, 1993.
Berry, E. and A. Miller-Pogacar (ed.), *Re-Entering the Sign*, Ann Arbor, MI, 1995.
Boym, Svetlana, *Common Places*, Cambridge, MA, and London, 1994.
Boym, Svetlana, *The Future of Nostalgia*, New York, 2002.
Condee, Nancy (ed.), *Soviet Hieroglyphics: Visual Culture in Late Twentieth-century Russia*, Bloomington and London, 1995.
Freidin, Gregory (ed.), *Russian Culture in Transition*, Stanford, CA, 1993.
Gillespie, David, *Russian Cinema*, London, 2003.
Horton, Andrew and Michael Brashinsky, *The Zero-Hour: Glasnost and Soviet Cinema in Transition*, Princeton, MA, 1991.
Kelly, C. and D. Shepherd (eds.), *Russian Cultural Studies: An Introduction*, Oxford, 1998.
Lawton, Anna, *Kinoglasnost*, Cambridge, 1992.
Shalin, Dmitry, *Russian Culture at the Crossroads*, Boulder, CO, and Oxford, 1996.

Websites

http://www.persons.ru/
http://ftp.nns.ru/persons/mihalkov.html
http://www.nns.ru/restricted/persons/mihalko0.html
http://www.whoiswho.ru/russian/Free/51998/mihalkovr.htm

www.ingramcontent.com/pod-product-compliance
Lightning Source LLC
Chambersburg PA
CBHW070737230426
43669CB00014B/2483